MW00459598

*classWorks 1 ***

# Banish Your Bookkeeping Nightmares

## The Go-To Guide for the Self-Employed to Save Money, Reduce Frustration, and Satisfy the IRS

# Lisa London, CPA

Deep River Press, Inc.

Sanford, North Carolina

The Accountant Beside You Presents
BANISH Your Bookkeeping Nightmares
ISBN 978-1-945561-07-8
Library of Congress Control Number 2017935070

Published by Deep River Press, Inc. March 2017
www.DeepRiver.press
Copyright 2017 Deep River Press, Inc.

All rights reserved. No portion of the contents of this book may be reproduced in any form or by any means without the written permission of the publisher unless otherwise noted.

Reasonable efforts have been made to assure the information in this book is reliable and complete. No representations or warranties are made for the accuracy or completeness of the contents of this book. Any responsibility for errors or omissions is disclaimed by the author.

Tax and regulatory requirements change and are specific to individual situations. No information in this book should be perceived as tax or legal advice. Any questions or requests for advice should directed to your personal tax advisor.

All trademarks herein are the property of their respective owners.
None of the companies are affiliated with this book or Deep River Press, Inc. and the inclusion in this book should not be construed as an endorsement.

EDITED BY Susan Sipal
COVER DESIGN BY Greg Schultz

## Other Books by Lisa London, CPA

*QuickBooks for Churches & Other Religious Organizations*

*Church Accounting: The How-To Guide for Small & Growing Churches*

*Using QuickBooks for Nonprofit Organizations, Associations, & Clubs*

*Using QuickBooks Online for Small Nonprofits & Churches*

*For my children,*
*Rachel, Adair, James, and Henry*

# Contents

# The BANISH System

Being self-employed brings forth a huge range of emotions: from the thrill of knowing you are in charge to the terror of that same knowledge, from the flexibility in your life to the long hours you never expected. You want to spend time following your dreams and making your business successful, not bogged down in the accounting.

That is where I can help. As a CPA, I have worked with all sizes of companies—garage start-ups to Fortune 500 level—as well as churches and nonprofits. I have worked as an auditor with one of the largest accounting firms in the world and as a director of finance in a large corporation. Along the way, I've consulted with mom and pop businesses, assisted venture-backed start-ups, and taught seminars and classes. When I was treasurer at my church, I stumbled into such a mess, it led me to create a series of books—**The Accountant Beside You**.

**The Accountant Beside You** resources assist non-accountants in managing finances without raising their stress level. This newest book, *BANISH Your Bookkeeping Nightmares,* takes you through the six steps of BANISH—**B**rief Yourself, **A**rrange Your Environment, **N**etwork Your Data, **I**mport Your Transactions, **S**ummarize Your Information, and **H**ead Into the Next Year.

You may think that the bookkeeping will be too much for you to handle. I promise it is not. I am a firm believer that you should do your own bookkeeping while your business is small so later, when your business has grown and you need to hire someone else to do it, you know what looks reasonable and what questions to ask. As you will see in some of the chapters, saying, "It's my accountant's fault" is not a legal defense.

I'll explain how to determine what information you need, how to organize it, how to choose an accounting system, how to automate where possible, and how to budget for the next year. You will also learn which expenses are deductible, and I'll step you through how to fill out various IRS forms.

You may also wish to check out my website, www.AccountantBesideYou.com for discussions, blog posts, helpful videos, and additional resources.

This book assumes you are self-employed, or as the IRS puts it, a Sole Proprietor. If your business is set up as a corporation (C-Corp, S-Corp, or LLC) or partnership, you will find most of the information helpful, but corporate taxes are beyond the scope of this book. Keep an eye on www.AccountantBesideYou.com for the latest releases.

Whether you're participating in the sharing economy as a host on Airbnb, opening an eBay store, working as a freelancer, running a home-based business, or any of the other myriad of self-employed options; let me help you save money, reduce frustration, and satisfy the IRS.

Let's get started.

*Look for these scrolls for useful tips and information.*
*For your convenience, I'll have a list of active hyperlinks to the IRS and other webpages I reference on www.AccountantBesideYou.com.*

*In 2009 Nicolas Cage owed $6.6 million to the IRS. He blamed his financial manager and claimed to be a victim. His manager blamed Cage's reckless spending.*

*The IRS didn't care whose fault it was. They and the state of Nevada foreclosed on Cage's multimillion-dollar home.*

# BANISH Step 1—Brief Yourself

Before you can streamline your bookkeeping, you need to know what data you'll need. That way, you'll know what data to gather, what to keep, and how best to report it.

## A. How Do You Know What You Need?

For this first section, I'm going to assume you're new to your business. Even if you are already familiar with this information, please read through it and think about any other financial data you will need to track.

The most common users of your financial data are:

- the IRS
- state agencies
- the bank (or any other lender)
- and YOU.

Each of these users have different needs and requirements. Let's review what type of information each may need.

### 1) Hobby or Business?

The first thing the IRS needs to know is whether your business is a *Hobby* or a *Business*. The biggest difference between these two designations is a *Business* can deduct losses, a *Hobby* cannot.

The IRS presumes a valid business if it makes a profit in three of the last five years (with exceptions for certain industries). See www.irs.gov/uac/is-your-hobby-a-for-profit-endeavor. If you are showing losses, the IRS will ask the following questions:

1. Do you behave as if you intend to make a profit?
   Considerable time and effort may show profit motive. You are not required to be full time, but it may be a good idea to keep a log of the effort you are making.
2. Do you keep complete and accurate records?
   If you don't already, you will after you finish this book.
3. Do you run the business the way a successful owner would?

If you can demonstrate that you adapt to a changing environment to improve profitability, the answer is yes.

4. Do you market and advertise consistently?
To show these things, prepare a business plan and revise it annually.

5. Do you have the knowledge to run this business?
You don't have to start with the expertise, but you must show you are trying to learn it.

6. Is there an expectation assets may appreciate in value?
Some business take a while before profit is seen. For example, if you grow Christmas trees, you assume the trees (the assets) will become more valuable as they get older (appreciate in value).

7. Have you made profits in similar activities in previous years?
This does not mean you must show you have already been successful, but if you have declared losses in a similar business in the past, it may point to a lack of determination. Remember however, lack of prior experience is not a factor.

8. Are any losses from circumstances beyond your control or from the startup?
Losses continuing past startup years may be an indication of an absence of profit motive, so the IRS will scrutinize harder. With proof the losses were beyond your control, you can show profit motive.

9. Do you depend on the income from the business?
If this is your only source of income, that is a good indicator of profit motive.

10. Does the business have elements of pleasure or recreation?
If you get personal pleasure out of the business, you can't blame the IRS for being more suspicious. An example of this may be a scuba diver who takes a few people out for a private dive to help pay for his boat.

The personal pleasure rule is not sufficient to rule out the profit motive, if the owner shows marketing efforts. This means you may also want to document the non-pleasurable parts of the job (i.e. cleaning the boat, changing vacation times to accommodate guest schedules, etc.).

If you believe your business would be classified as a hobby, you will record the income on IRS Form 1040—Other Income (Line 21 as of the date of writing). If you itemize deductions, add the related expenses (no greater than the income) on Schedule A—Other Miscellaneous Deductions (Line 28).

## Bottom Line
*If you are collecting money to help offset your recreational expenses, treat it as a hobby.*

For purposes of this book, I'm going to assume you are focusing on being successful and would pass the IRS determinations as a business. We'll start with reviewing the minimum information the IRS requires. I'll go over these in detail in later chapters, but first let's look at some of the forms.

### 2. Form 1040, Schedule C—Profit or Loss From Business

This is where you will show your income and detail the expenses each year.

| SCHEDULE C (Form 1040) | Profit or Loss From Business (Sole Proprietorship) | OMB No. 1545-0074 **2016** |
|---|---|---|
| Department of the Treasury Internal Revenue Service (99) | ▶ Information about Schedule C and its separate instructions is at *www.irs.gov/schedulec*. ▶ Attach to Form 1040, 1040NR, or 1041; partnerships generally must file Form 1065. | Attachment Sequence No. **09** |

| Name of proprietor | | Social security number (SSN) |
|---|---|---|

**A** Principal business or profession, including product or service (see instructions) — **B** Enter code from instructions ▶

**C** Business name. If no separate business name, leave blank. — **D** Employer ID number (EIN), (see instr.)

**E** Business address (including suite or room no.) ▶
City, town or post office, state, and ZIP code

**F** Accounting method: (1) ☐ Cash (2) ☐ Accrual (3) ☐ Other (specify) ▶

**G** Did you "materially participate" in the operation of this business during 2016? If "No," see instructions for limit on losses. ☐ Yes ☐ No

**H** If you started or acquired this business during 2016, check here . . . . . . . . . ▶ ☐

**I** Did you make any payments in 2016 that would require you to file Form(s) 1099? (see instructions) . . . . ☐ Yes ☐ No

**J** If "Yes," did you or will you file required Forms 1099? . . . . . . . . . . . . . . ☐ Yes ☐ No

**Part I  Income**

| | | |
|---|---|---|
| 1 | Gross receipts or sales. See instructions for line 1 and check the box if this income was reported to you on Form W-2 and the "Statutory employee" box on that form was checked . . . . . . ▶ ☐ | 1 |
| 2 | Returns and allowances . . . . . . . . . . . . . . . . . . . . . | 2 |
| 3 | Subtract line 2 from line 1 . . . . . . . . . . . . . . . . . . . | 3 |
| 4 | Cost of goods sold (from line 42) . . . . . . . . . . . . . . . . | 4 |
| 5 | Gross profit. Subtract line 4 from line 3 . . . . . . . . . . . . . | 5 |
| 6 | Other income, including federal and state gasoline or fuel tax credit or refund (see instructions) . . . | 6 |
| 7 | Gross income. Add lines 5 and 6 . . . . . . . . . . . . . . . . ▶ | 7 |

**Part II  Expenses.** Enter expenses for business use of your home **only** on line 30.

| | | | | | | |
|---|---|---|---|---|---|---|
| 8 | Advertising . . . . . | 8 | | 18 | Office expense (see instructions) | 18 |
| 9 | Car and truck expenses (see instructions). . . . . | 9 | | 19 | Pension and profit-sharing plans . | 19 |
| 10 | Commissions and fees . | 10 | | 20 | Rent or lease (see instructions): | |
| 11 | Contract labor (see instructions) | 11 | | a | Vehicles, machinery, and equipment | 20a |
| 12 | Depletion . . . | 12 | | b | Other business property . . . | 20b |
| 13 | Depreciation and section 179 expense deduction (not included in Part III) (see instructions). . . . . | 13 | | 21 | Repairs and maintenance . . . | 21 |
| | | | | 22 | Supplies (not included in Part III) . | 22 |
| | | | | 23 | Taxes and licenses . . . . | 23 |
| | | | | 24 | Travel, meals, and entertainment: | |
| 14 | Employee benefit programs (other than on line 19) . . | 14 | | a | Travel . . . . . . . | 24a |
| 15 | Insurance (other than health) | 15 | | b | Deductible meals and entertainment (see instructions) . | 24b |
| 16 | Interest: | | | 25 | Utilities . . . . . . | 25 |
| a | Mortgage (paid to banks, etc.) | 16a | | 26 | Wages (less employment credits). | 26 |
| b | Other . . . . | 16b | | 27a | Other expenses (from line 48) . | 27a |
| 17 | Legal and professional services | 17 | | b | Reserved for future use . . . | 27b |

| | | | |
|---|---|---|---|
| 28 | Total expenses before expenses for business use of home. Add lines 8 through 27a . . . . . ▶ | 28 | |
| 29 | Tentative profit or (loss). Subtract line 28 from line 7 . . . . . . . . . . . . . | 29 | |
| 30 | Expenses for business use of your home. Do not report these expenses elsewhere. Attach Form 8829 unless using the simplified method (see instructions). Simplified method filers only: enter the total square footage of: (a) your home: _____ and (b) the part of your home used for business: _____. Use the Simplified Method Worksheet in the instructions to figure the amount to enter on line 30 . . . . . . | 30 | |
| 31 | Net profit or (loss). Subtract line 30 from line 29. • If a profit, enter on both Form 1040, line 12 (or Form 1040NR, line 13) and on Schedule SE, line 2. (If you checked the box on line 1, see instructions). Estates and trusts, enter on Form 1041, line 3. • If a loss, you must go to line 32. | 31 | |
| 32 | If you have a loss, check the box that describes your investment in this activity (see instructions). • If you checked 32a, enter the loss on both Form 1040, line 12, (or Form 1040NR, line 13) and on Schedule SE, line 2. (If you checked the box on line 1, see the line 31 instructions). Estates and trusts, enter on Form 1041, line 3. • If you checked 32b, you must attach Form 6198. Your loss may be limited. | 32a ☐ All investment is at risk. 32b ☐ Some investment is not at risk. | |

| For Paperwork Reduction Act Notice, see the separate instructions. | Cat. No. 11334P | Schedule C (Form 1040) 2016 |
|---|---|---|

The net profit or loss then is added to your Form 1040. I'll take you through each of the line items in Step 5, but for now, note the various types of categories the IRS is interested in. You'll learn how to set up your bookkeeping system to make filling out this form much less painful in Step 4.

### 3. Form 1040 ES—Self-Employment Quarterly Estimated Taxes

Because you're not receiving a regular paycheck from your business, you must estimate how much income you expect to make and calculate the federal income and employment taxes. As you are the employer, you must pay both the employer and employee portions of the Social Security and Medicare taxes.

| **2017 Estimated Tax Worksheet** | | *Keep for Your Records* | | |
|---|---|---|---|---|
| 1 | Adjusted gross income you expect in 2017 (see instructions) . . . . . . . . . . | **1** | | |
| 2 | • If you plan to itemize deductions, enter the estimated total of your itemized deductions. **Caution:** *If line 1 is over $156,900 your deduction may be reduced. See Pub. 505 for details.* | | | |
| | • If you do not plan to itemize deductions, enter your standard deduction. | **2** | | |
| 3 | Subtract line 2 from line 1. | **3** | | |
| 4 | Exemptions. Multiply $4,050 by the number of personal exemptions. **Caution:** *See Worksheet 2-6 in Pub. 505 to figure the amount to enter if line 1 is over: $156,900* . . | **4** | | |
| 5 | Subtract line 4 from line 3 | **5** | | |
| 6 | **Tax.** Figure your tax on the amount on line 5 by using the **2017 Tax Rate Schedules.** **Caution:** *If you will have qualified dividends or a net capital gain, or expect to exclude or deduct foreign earned income or housing, see Worksheets 2-7 and 2-8 in Pub. 505 to figure the tax.* . . | **6** | | |
| 7 | Alternative minimum tax from **Form 6251** or included on **Form 1040A, line 28** . . . . . . . | **7** | | |
| 8 | Add lines 6 and 7. Add to this any other taxes you expect to include in the total on Form 1040, line 44 . . . . . . . . . . . . . . . . . . . . . . . . | **8** | | |
| 9 | Credits (see instructions). **Do not** include any income tax withholding on this line . . . . . . | **9** | | |
| 10 | Subtract line 9 from line 8. If zero or less, enter -0- . . . . . . . . . . . . | **10** | | |
| 11 | Self-employment tax (see instructions) . . . . . . . . . . . . . . . . | **11** | | |
| 12 | Other taxes (see instructions) . . . . . . . . . . . . . . . . . | **12** | | |
| 13a | Add lines 10 through 12 . . . . . . . . . . . . . . . . . . | **13a** | | |
| b | Earned income credit, additional child tax credit, fuel tax credit, net premium tax credit, refundable American opportunity credit, and refundable credit from Form 8885 . . . . . . . | **13b** | | |
| c | **Total 2017 estimated tax.** Subtract line 13b from line 13a. If zero or less, enter -0- . . . ▶ | **13c** | | |
| 14a | Multiply line 13c by 90% (66²/₃% for farmers and fishermen) . . . . | **14a** | | |
| b | Required annual payment based on prior year's tax (see instructions) . | **14b** | | |
| c | **Required annual payment to avoid a penalty.** Enter the **smaller** of line 14a or 14b . . . ▶ | **14c** | | |
| | **Caution:** *Generally, if you do not prepay (through income tax withholding and estimated tax payments) at least the amount on line 14c, you may owe a penalty for not paying enough estimated tax. To avoid a penalty, make sure your estimate on line 13c is as accurate as possible. Even if you pay the required annual payment, you may still owe tax when you file your return. If you prefer, you can pay the amount shown on line 13c. For details, see chapter 2 of Pub. 505.* | | | |
| 15 | Income tax withheld and estimated to be withheld during 2017 (including income tax withholding on pensions, annuities, certain deferred income, etc.) . . . . . . . . . . . | **15** | | |
| 16a | Subtract line 15 from line 14c . . . . . . . . . . | **16a** | | |
| | Is the result zero or less? | | | |
| | ☐ **Yes.** Stop here. You are not required to make estimated tax payments. | | | |
| | ☐ **No.** Go to line 16b. | | | |
| b | Subtract line 15 from line 13c . . . . . . . . . . | **16b** | | |
| | Is the result less than $1,000? | | | |
| | ☐ **Yes.** Stop here. You are not required to make estimated tax payments. | | | |

### *BANISH Bite #1*
*Open a separate bank account and get a separate credit card for your business. It will make it easier to keep your records organized.*

Use current B of A so Cely for auts
Use another account for personal
expenses, like medical.
consider ACH checking w/ debit card

*have not had to pay because of* RMD *for* pled, *KPERS* SS *Tax* deduc

## 4. Form 1040 SE—Self-Employment Taxes Annual Filing

After the end of the year, you fill out this form to reconcile your quarterly payments with your actual taxes due. There are two versions of this form, the Short Schedule SE and the Long Schedule SE. (The Short Schedule is pictured.)

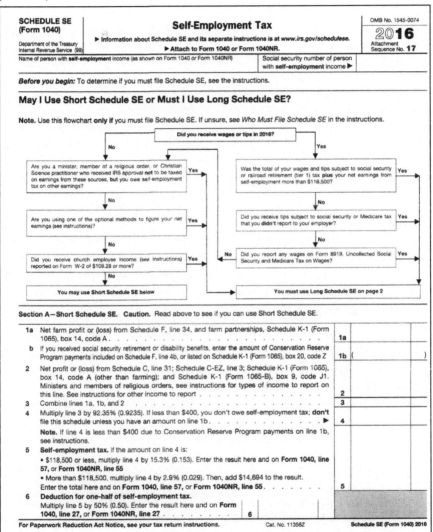

## 5. Forms 1099 MISC—Miscellaneous Income and 1099 K

This form is sent from businesses to independent contractors if they were paid over a certain amount each year. If you hire other people to help you with your business, you may need to send these. If you offer free-lance services or are a writer who receives royalty checks, you may receive these.

*Receive 1K2 + possible Amazon*
*Send to NP*

*Square will send 1099*

If you sell products or services through a credit card processor, you'll receive a 1099K. I'll go over 1099s in more detail in Step 5.

Those are the primary forms required by the IRS. If you have a tax return from last year, review it to see what additional information you will need.

| PAYER'S name, street address, city or town, state or province, country, ZIP or foreign postal code, and telephone no. | | 1 Rents $ | OMB No. 1545-0115 | Miscellaneous Income |
|---|---|---|---|---|
| | | 2 Royalties $ | 20**17** Form **1099-MISC** | |
| | | 3 Other income $ | 4 Federal income tax withheld $ | Copy A |
| PAYER'S federal identification number | RECIPIENT'S identification number | 5 Fishing boat proceeds $ | 6 Medical and health care payments $ | For Internal Revenue Service Center |
| RECIPIENT'S name | | 7 Nonemployee compensation $ | 8 Substitute payments in lieu of dividends or interest $ | File with Form 1096. For Privacy Act and Paperwork Reduction Act Notice, see the |
| Street address (including apt. no.) | | 9 Payer made direct sales of $5,000 or more of consumer products to a buyer (recipient) for resale ▶ ☐ | 10 Crop insurance proceeds $ | 2017 General Instructions for Certain Information Returns. |
| City or town, state or province, country, and ZIP or foreign postal code | | 11 | 12 | |
| Account number (see instructions) | FATCA filing requirement ☐ | 2nd TIN not. ☐ | 13 Excess golden parachute payments $ | 14 Gross proceeds paid to an attorney $ |
| 15a Section 409A deferrals $ | 15b Section 409A income $ | 16 State tax withheld $ | 17 State/Payer's state no. | 18 State income $ |

Form **1099-MISC**    Cat. No. 14425J    www.irs.gov/form1099misc    Department of the Treasury - Internal Revenue Service

**Do Not Cut or Separate Forms on This Page — Do Not Cut or Separate Forms on This Page**

## B. State Required Forms   *do research*

Each state has different requirements for filings. At www.accountantbesideyou.com/state-weblinks, I have active links to each of the states' Departments of Revenue and Secretaries of State. Please review your state's requirements, looking especially at:

- Income tax
- Sales tax
- Business licenses (also check to see if your municipality has any requirements)
- Business filing requirements. Most states' Secretary of State sites have a "Start a new business" link that details what is required in your area.

## C. Bank or Other Lender Requirements

If you have borrowed money to get your business off the ground or plan on borrowing money in the future, you will be required to submit financial statements or cash flow projections. I'll show you how to design these reports in Step 5. — *money borrowed thru CC, 0% interest*

## D.  What do YOU Need to Run Your Business?

This is the most important question of all. If you don't have the information you need to run your business well, chances are you won't be around long enough to worry about all these other forms.

It's hard to know what you don't know, right? Think about these questions.

1.  What information will be helpful for you to run and grow your business?
2.  Do you know your cash status? *yes*
3.  Which products or services sell best? Which are slowest?
4.  Will you be issuing invoices to customers? Do they need to be done on site or from your office? *don't know*
5.  Do you need quick access to customer names and numbers? *yes*
6.  Which expenses have increased?
7.  Is revenue trending up or down?

I'll explain how to use the basic financial reports to help you. Then you'll need to consider the information you use on a daily, weekly, or monthly basis. Jot down some thoughts, and as we work through the book, think about how you'll use what you are learning to get that information most efficiently.

## E.  A Quick Accounting Lesson (I promise it won't be painful.)

There are some basic accounting terms you need to know. I've included a glossary of the most common ones in the back of the book, but I need you to understand a few things before we begin.

The three main things accountants love to talk about are **Assets, Liabilities,** and **Equity**. Our world seems to revolve around them. Basically, **Assets** are things you own or are owed to you. This includes the bank and investment accounts, accounts receivable, buildings, furniture, and equipment. It can also include expenses you've paid for but not yet used, like prepaid insurance or prepaid postage.

**Liabilities** are what you owe. The mortgage to the bank, the credit card bill, payroll due to employees, and payroll taxes due to the government are all liabilities.

**Equity** is what is left, which is why accounting is considered a Balanced Equation.

*Assets = Liabilities + Equity*

*or*

*Assets — Liabilities = Equity*

Poppy Davis, CPA, sums up the accounting terms wonderfully in her *Small Nonprofits QuickBooks Primer*. I've changed the wording slightly.

> **Assets stick around—Expenses go away.** If you buy a stove, it sticks around, so it is an asset. If you hire a repairman to fix the stove, he goes away, so the repair cost is an expense.

> **Income is yours—Liabilities belong to others.** If you receive money for a service you provided, it is income; but if you borrow money from the bank to build a new kitchen, it is a liability.

> **Owner's Equity** is what is left over for you.

Other important financial terms include Income, Cost of Goods Sold, Gross Profit, and Expenses.

**Income** is the money you sell your products or services for. The IRS asks for your "Gross receipts or sales." For example, assume you are a writer and sell your books at signings and shows. If you sold 100 books at $10.00 per book, your gross receipt is $1000.00.

**Cost of Goods Sold (COGS)** is the actual cost to produce the product you sold. The Cost of Goods Sold is the price you paid for the book plus the shipping. Using the example above, if you pay the printer $5.00 for the book and $1.00 to ship it, the COGS is $6.00 for one book. If you sell 100 books, your COGS will be $600.00.

**Gross Profit** is the difference between the gross receipts or sales and the cost of goods sold. With sales of $1000 and COGS of $600, your gross profit would be $400 ($1000-$600).

**Expenses** are the remaining costs of running your business that are not specific to the individual sales of a product or service (those are in COGS).

### F. Cash vs Accrual Methods of Recording Income and Expenses

There are two methods to track revenues and expenses in the accounting world—Cash and Accrual.

The **Cash Method** is the simplest. The cash is recorded in the financial statements when it is physically received and deducted when the checks are written.

The **Accrual Method** requires dating the transaction when the income was earned (i.e. when you did the work for a client or entered into a contract), not when you received the money. Expenses are recorded when ordered, not when you pay for them.

The accrual method gives you the most accurate financial picture of your business; showing money you have earned and expenses you have incurred.

The cash basis gives you a better idea of when the money has come in or gone out. Some accounting systems allow you to run reports both ways.

Whichever method you use must be consistent on your annual tax return. If you are using the cash method, pay special attention to what bills are paid before year-end. An invoice paid on December 31 may be deductible for the current year; but if you wait until January 1st, it would not be deductible until the next year's tax return.

### G. Financial Reports

There are three standard financial reports:
1. Balance Sheet
2. Income Statement
3. Statement of Cash Flow.

I'm giving you quick definitions now, but we will see these in detail as we set up your system.

The **Balance Sheet** reflects the overall health of your business. It's a snapshot in time of the amount of cash in the bank and the value of the other assets, offset by the amounts owed to others.

The **Income Statement** shows how much you have sold and what it costs to run your business over a period of time. This should be reviewed at least monthly and compared to previous months and the previous year to see trends.

The **Statement of Cash Flow** shows you where your money comes from (customers versus lenders) and where it went (payment of expenses or reduction of debt).

Listed below are other management reports you may need and what they are used for:

**Comparison to Budget**—to see if you are achieving your financial goals.

**Accounts Receivable Aging**—shows how much money your customers owe you and how long has it been unpaid.

**Accounts Payable Outstanding**—alerts you to when bills are due, so you can plan your cash needs.

**Sales by Customer**—shows who your significant customers are so you can follow up accordingly.

**Sales by Product/Service**—details what is selling and what isn't.

We'll use these reports and forms to set up your accounting system. Before starting, let's go to Step 2 and organize your information.

***BANISH Action Steps:***

- *Determine if you are running a business or just a hobby.*
- *Pull together the forms and information required by the IRS, State, Municipality, and Lenders.*
- *Consider the type of information you need to grow your business.*
- *Understand basic accounting terms and reports.*

*Taxpayers owe actor George M. Cohan a debt of gratitude. He was notoriously bad at keeping receipts and appealed the loss of the deductions to the tax courts.*

*The courts sided with him and now the Cohan Rule allows taxpayers to deduct **some** of their reasonable business-related expenses even if the receipts have been lost.*

## BANISH Step 2—Arrange Your Environment (Organize Your Business For Quick Results)

Before you start recording your transactions to generate useful information, you need to know what data you have, how to access it, and how to keep track of it. While we all may wish to be a "paperless society," most of us aren't quite there yet. I'll show you how to organize both your electronic records and your paper records. You can then mix and match these techniques to see which works best for you.

### BANISH Bite # 2
*The First Rule of Organizing Your Records:*
*Keep It as Simple as Possible.*

Don't let yourself get overwhelmed before you even get started. For now, don't worry about all the old documents and files. Let's focus on setting up the system going forward.

### A. Computer Organization

Computers—those things that save so much time and yet cause us so much trouble. Computer filing systems (or lack thereof) can be just as frustrating as the loose papers around your office. How many times have we searched our computer, not remembering how the file was labeled or which of the thousands of file folders we may have put it in?

I'm going to show you how to use your computer and automation to save lots of time with your bookkeeping. With that efficiency comes the need for security and backups. The last thing you want is to set up the perfect system with all your data and have your system go down without a backup.

I like to use a cloud storage account that automatically saves any document I'm working on to both my computer and the internet. That way, if my hard drive crashes, I haven't lost all my work. But with this convenience comes the security risk of having your financial data online. You can't make yourself immune from hackers, but you *can* make their work a lot harder.

Design passwords with special characters (#$%*) and stay away from birthdays, children's names, or any information people could gleam from your Facebook account. I personally have an easy-to-remember password for non-financial, unimportant websites that is vastly different than the password I use for financial institutions.

Let's get started by setting up a Google Drive, OneDrive, Dropbox, or any other free (or paid) cloud storage account. These programs allow you to work offline if your internet is down, and then they will automatically sync the files once access is secured.

First, set up a primary folder in your business name (or however you refer to it). Then, under the primary folder, set up the following folders:

**Legal** (i.e. My Business–Legal) This will hold electronic copies of any state, local, or federal licensing documents, your EIN (Employers Identification Number) if you have one, your state or city sales tax ID number, and any other legal documents. Feel free to add subfolders as needed.

**Insurance** (i.e. My Business–Insurance) Save your insurance policies here—car, business, health, etc.

**Year** (i.e. My Business–2017) The **Year** folder will be for your transactions that occur in that particular year. It will include subfolders to keep the transactions organized. Each year, you will want to set up a new folder and the related subfolders.

Under the **Year** folder, set up the following subfolders as the basics. Later, add more folders that are specific to your business as you need to, but try to keep them as broad as possible. Label them in such a way that you will understand what is in the files, and be as consistent as possible.

---

### BANISH Bite # 3
*Develop your own naming protocol to make searching for files easier.*
*Bank statements could be "BS-17-Jan", "BS-17-Feb".*

---

**Bank Statements**—for your monthly bank statements and related reconciliations.

**Credit Card Statements**—for your monthly statements and related reconciliations. And, yes, you need to reconcile credit card statements just like bank statements.

**Credit Card Receipts**—for emailed, electronic, and photo receipts. You may wish to set up subfolders for each month if you use your credit card frequently.

### BANISH Bite # 4

*Use the camera on your phone to take a picture of a receipt as soon as you receive it. (Some credit card companies have apps to automatically match the receipts to the statement). Then save the picture to the appropriate subfolder using the naming protocol you've developed. Now you don't have to worry about losing the receipt.*

**Income**—for emails or electronic reports of money earned. For example, your Airbnb, Uber, eBay, or royalty statements would be saved here.

**Bills**—for emailed, electronic, and photos of invoices. Set up subfolders for each month.

**IRS**—for any electronic copies of IRS forms or correspondence. Set up subfolders for each type of tax return, Federal, Self-Employment, and 1099s. I'd recommend setting up a separate file for IRS Correspondence. Though the IRS does not communicate with taxpayers through email, it's a good idea to scan all correspondence and save the digital copy here. If you don't have a scanner, take a picture with your phone and save it to the Correspondence file.

**State Tax and Licensing**—for any state or local tax documents and licenses correspondence.

**Accounting System Backups**—In the next chapter, we'll talk about setting up accounting systems. You'll want to back up on a frequent basis to this folder.

**Customer Correspondence**—add subfolders by customer if this is frequent.

**Expense/Mileage/Travel Reports**—add monthly subfolders if you use these a lot.

I've kept the categories broad, so you don't have to go deep searching for things. Switch them around and add others as needed for your business.

> ## BANISH Bite # 5
> *Don't save any files to the Primary folder. There should be a subfolder related to the topic to use.*

### B. Office Organization

Your computer files are now ready to use, it's time to look at that desk.

Start by clearing off your desk completely. Put all that stuff in the other room for now.

Put your computer or laptop, monitors, printer, speakers, etc. back on the desk. Do you like the clean counter space? Before you add anything back, ask yourself, "Does it have to be on my desk? Is there a better place to store it?"

Now add back the absolute necessities one at a time. For me, it looks like this:

Phone stand that charges my phone; a small pottery vase that holds a couple of pens, pencils, and highlighter; a notebook; Post-it notes; and scratch paper.

On my wall hangs a file folder holder with three slots. In one slot are folders labeled Bills to Pay and Checks to Deposit; in the second is Things to Read; and the third holds my mailing labels for shipping books. When the mail comes, all the business items go in one of those folders, are filed, or are sent straight to the trashcan. If I lay it on my desk, it will just get piled in with other things and never handled.

Now you have a clear desk to work at. As a writer, I use this space to spread out the research I'm working on. Or perhaps, for your ecommerce business, you now have an area to fill sales orders.

Oops, all that other paperwork that was on your desk still needs to be handled. For the items that are not electronic, or for which you want to also keep a paper copy, I like Terressa Pierce's approach from www.FreeChurchForms.com. Whether you are in an established office or working out of your car, an organized system of paperwork will give you the data you need as efficiently as possible. Drawing upon Terressa's vast experience, I am paraphrasing (with her permission) an article from her website.

Setting up an organized file system takes a little time at first, but you will save enormous amounts of time later.

1. **Plan and Prepare**—If your filing system isn't working for you, then it's time to plan and create a truly effective system. Putting labels on your folders helps, but this alone will not work. Don't worry about needing anything special; just have on hand several colors of 2/5 cut tab folders, some hanging folders, and file labels.

2. **Create Broad File Categories**—Start sorting your documents into broad categories from your current file system or from that pile of papers on your desk. (The one you have been meaning to file for months.) And don't focus on details of your filing system right now. We'll worry about details later.

3. **Subcategorize**—After you have all your broad file categories (documents) in piles, pick one of them and sort through it again. This time break your paper down into smaller subcategories. Example: "Bills" could be divided into Tax Categories. If you have vendors you do a lot of transactions with, give them their own folder.

4. **Color Code Each Major Category**—Assign each major or broad category of paperwork a different color, and put each subcategory into that color of file folder. Use one hanging file to hold each set of colored folders. Example: "Bills" hanging file might be yellow, and each of your sub files will have a separate yellow file folder. This might seem strange, but color-coding your file system will save you precious time in filing and retrieving your papers. Imagine seeing all your folders filled with paperwork broken down by color. They are stacked neatly in hanging folders, and, because you know what color your "Bills" file is,

your hand naturally reaches for the correct part of your file drawer. Now that's organization!

5. **Create Labels**—Once you have the files color coded, label each subcategory. Label one hanging folder per each major category by name. I personally like labels that fold over the top so you can see from the front, top, or back of the folder. To make them easier to read, print them from your computer. Do not create a label called "Visa" for your subcategory folder credit card, because if you have more than one credit card they will be separated. Keep them together by creating labels called "Credit Card: Visa." Now when you create more folders for credit cards, they will be all together.

6. **File Documents into Your Filing Drawer**—This is your last step! All that is left is to place your files within each major category in alphabetical order in hanging folders, placing as many folders as possible in each hanging folder without overcrowding. Make your color folders line up as straight as possible in the drawer for easy reading.

When the time comes to find a document or to put something in a folder, look first for the correct major category by color and then by label.

With an organized file system, it's easy to put your hands on the correct file without a lot of searching.

As you can see, Terressa is passionate about her mission. Check out her site www.FreeChurchForms.com for other great administrative and organizing tips—even if you aren't a working for a church.

---

### BANISH Bite #6

*You are more likely to keep your records organized if you keep your filing system as simple as possible.*

---

### C. Car/Mobile Organization

As an entrepreneur, I'm in the car a lot. Whether I'm picking up the mail, calling on bookstores, or attending meetings, I often end up with loose papers in the car that need to be handled. Let's banish that nightmare with a few simple steps. First, get a thin plastic accordion file for under $10 that will hold up to letter sized paper.

Next, label the first five pockets as follows:

**Deposits**—hold checks received from customers and deposit receipts here. Take a picture of the checks before depositing to have the detail of the deposit available when you get back to your office.

**Bills**—place bills received from vendors or through the mail here to keep safe until you input them in your accounting system.

**Credit Card**—your receipts are filed here after you notate what the business purpose was and take a picture of them.

**To Read**—this may be brochures, flyers, or correspondence— anything you need to read when you get back to your office. If you don't need to read it—toss it! There is no need to handle it again if you'll never read it.

**Coupons**—Because you'll have this accordion file in your car or briefcase, you'll have your paper coupons available with you when you get to the office supply store.

The remaining pockets are available for you to personalize.

Carry it with you in your briefcase or in your car at all times, so you won't be pulling crumpled receipts and checks out of your purse or pocket and wonder what they were for. If the letter-sized file is too big, see if the envelope size is sufficient.

On your bookkeeping day, which I'll explain later, bring in your portable file and handle each of the items.

### BANISH Bite #7

*If you spend most of your time out of the office, keep an accordion file (with sections labeled) in your car or briefcase to hold checks to be deposited, deposit slips, receipts, business cards, mail, bills, etc.*

### D. Record Retention Guidelines

How long should you keep all these documents that are on your computer and in your file cabinets? Let's review your record retention needs.

#### 1) Normal, everyday financial documents—3 to 7 years

The basic IRS rules require you to keep most records three years and all employment tax records at least four years after the date the tax is paid. If the IRS finds fraud, they can go back seven years for an audit.

IRS agents are trained to differentiate fraud from "stupid" mistakes. But as you may not know if someone in your organization is committing fraud, it is a good idea to keep the financial data for the full seven years and includes invoices, bank statements, cancelled checks or scans of the checks, employee reimbursements, and audit reports.

---

### BANISH Bite #8
*When you box up your paper files, ALWAYS notate a "Dispose Of" date on the box.*

---

### 2) Titles, vital records, pension documents—Forever

There are a few things that should be kept pretty much forever. These include: titles to property, any legal documents, vital records, and retirement and pension records.

If you think it's important, save it. Your permanent documents should be kept in a fire-proof safe or safety deposit box.

### 3) Long-term assets-three years after disposal or pay off of mortgage

For mortgage, purchase records, contracts—three years after disposal of property or termination of contract.

Some documents need to be retained for an extended period as they pertain to long-term assets. Property records, i.e. mortgage documents, and equipment and other property purchase records should be kept for at least three years after you dispose of the property or pay off the loans. Check with your bank or insurer as they may have other guidelines.

### 4) Employment records—seven years after termination

Employment records should be kept for at least seven years after the employee leaves and MUST be kept in a locked, secure location. Your employment files should include:

Applications for employment
W-4 forms for each employee
Performance appraisal and evaluation forms
Employee handbook
Immigration I-9 form.

You may not have employees yet, but when you do, be prepared.

## E. Email and Other Electronic Information

If you've elected to have your bills and banks statements sent electronically, you don't have to print them out to save them. You are required to have access to the information for the three to seven years, so just download the files into its appropriate folder as discussed earlier.

**BANISH Bite # 9**

*Set up an email account to use only for business. If family or friends send messages to it, request they use your personal email.*

Emails may be the curse of our civilization. Trying to keep a handle on them is challenging.

Having a separate business email that you NEVER use for personal reasons will keep the time you spend scanning email to a minimum.

If your email program (like Outlook) allows you to set up files and rules, have any emailed bills go automatically to a Bills folder. Other suggested files are: Customer Correspondence (or specific customer names if there is a lot of communication), To Read (emails from useful organizations or associations or newsletters you subscribe to), and Consultants (for messages from your web designer, editor, or freelancers). Add more that are relevant to your business, but don't add so many it is difficult to find anything.

Once you have set up the rules to move emails from recurring people and businesses into the above files, your inbox is now down to primarily promotional materials and spam. Scan through it quickly, move and set up new rules for important emails, and then highlight and delete the rest.

Organizing your electronic data doesn't help if it can be lost with a corrupted hard drive. A cloud-based system like Google Drive or Dropbox will backup any data on the computer files to the internet as you save them. As an extra precaution, I recommend backing up the financial system and all electronic statements to a flash drive after the end of each year. Clearly mark the flash drive with the contents and store in a fire-proof safe or safety deposit box.

Now it's time to see how to put this all together in an accounting system.

### BANISH Action Steps

- *Open a cloud-based storage account.*
- *Setup a primary business folder on your computer, and under the primary folder, add folders for Legal, Insurance, and the Year.*
- *Set up your physical file folders.*
- *Purchase an accordion file for your car or briefcase.*
- *File/store old documents with the proper disposal date listed.*
- *Establish your email rules so emailed bills, invoices, and statements go to specific, recognizable folders.*

*Martha Stewart failed to pay over $200,000 of taxes on her New York home. She claimed she spent very little time there, so she didn't think she had to pay taxes.*

*The New York tax authorities disagreed.*

# BANISH Step 3-Network Your Data

You will save time by automating as much of the bookkeeping work as possible. Because everyone's situation is different, I'll explain options that save time but cost money, and others that are free or very low cost that take a bit more time. You can mix and match these to work for your situation.

Please note: I'll examine a variety of products. As of the writing of this, I do not receive any remuneration from any of the related companies. Because new products are coming out all the time, I may mention some I have not yet used, but are receiving good reviews. And just because I find it easy to use, you may not. I highly recommend using the free trials any time you are considering purchasing a product.

## A.  Desktop or Online?

There are so many options for accounting systems. No longer must you be professionally trained in accounting and tied to your desk. The programs are fairly intuitive and easy to access.

But with the additional options, comes more decisions. Do I want to keep all my bookkeeping together in one place, securely locked behind a door? Do I need to access reports, transfer money, and invoice customers in the field?

Deciding whether to use a computer-based or an internet-based system primarily revolves around the following questions:

**What is the cost?** Is it a one-time price to buy the program and use until it is no longer supported or no longer fits your needs? Or is it a monthly subscription that is updated automatically as enhancements are designed? If you don't have elaborate needs, a desktop version of a program may work for years, saving money in the long run.

**Do you have consistent internet access?** If you are lucky enough to live in a community with Google Fiber, this may not be an issue. If your internet service often slows or goes down, using an online accounting system will be very frustrating.

**What is the vulnerability to unauthorized access?** This is important whether you use an online system or work on your desktop. Do you use strong passwords and keep your system up to date with anti-virus software? Is the company that runs the online system reputable? Have their customers been hacked? What is your comfort level?

**How important is mobile access?** If you work primarily in the field and need the information immediately, an online option will be better.

**Is the reporting adequate?** Generally, the online programs do not have as strong reporting capabilities as the desktop versions. If you want to customize information, this should be evaluated for any of the systems you are considering.

Some of the desktop programs also offer a mobile app to give you some of the flexibility of the online option. Bottom line is you must decide what fits in your budget and will work best for you.

### BANISH Bite # 10

*Anytime you are considering an online product that will hold your financial data, you need to understand their privacy settings and terms of service.*

*Pay special attention to what happens to the data if you quit using the system and if it is possible to save the data on your own system. If the company goes out of business, can you get your data?*

### B. Lower Cost, but Takes More Time Options

You can always go old school with a notebook, pencil, calculator, and envelopes. My mother used to keep our farm books this way, with columns titled *Money In* and *Money Out*. I really don't recommend this approach. Besides being time consuming, it's prone to errors and won't give you reports to help run your business.

The next least expensive option is a spreadsheet on your computer. It has the advantage of ease of use, but it can be time consuming to set up, data entry is tedious, and due to the human set up factor, it's also prone to error. The reporting is limited by the amount of time you want to spend programing the spreadsheet.

If you only a have a few expenses to track, I have a basic spreadsheet accounting program available at my website, www.AccountantBesideYou.com.

It will track up to ten revenue accounts and up to forty different types of expenses in a general ledger format and gives you monthly, quarterly, and annual income statements.

You then manually input the checks you have written and deposits made, and the system will total them for you by business unit (in case you have more than one). Here is an example screen shot.

The inputs will then be summarized in reports. Here is an example of the Profit and Loss Statement.

Spreadsheets are a very inexpensive and viable option if you only have a few transactions each month. For example, if you rent out a room online and only receive a few cash transfers a month from Airbnb, manually inputting the information will be easy. If you have a landscaping service with several clients to bill and lots of different expenses, the spreadsheet option will probably be too cumbersome.

Another option is a free online accounting package. The most common free personal program is www.Mint.com. Mint will allow you to track your financial data online and is useful for budgeting. There are no business specific options, like invoicing available. It does not have customer support and you cannot reconcile the bank accounts.

As a free service, they make money by offering you "ways to save" for referral fees and ad banners.

Another example is www.Waveapps.com. It is a basic program that allows you to download the transactions from your bank and credit card companies. You then categorize the expenses and sales and run reports. Wave also offers an app that allows you to take a picture of your receipt and then upload it into your system with a 70% accuracy. Because it's a free service, the company will display ads to sign up for their credit card and payroll services.

The free services give you the convenience of the automation, but requires you to do additional research to see if the companies are reputable and have a strong likelihood of being around.

## C. Saves Time, But Costs a Bit More

There are many good accounting packages developed by companies who have been in the business for a long while. Each company has a range of products with features for different types and levels of businesses.

For example, if you run an e-commerce site with physical products, you may need a system that tracks inventory. If you are a hair stylist, you probably want a system that will track your clients. For free-lancers with long term projects, a job-costing option would be useful.

I'll go through some of the options of the most well-known accounting programs to show you the differences, but you'll need to compare your needs to their capabilities to make a final decision.

Probably the most well-known personal accounting program is Quicken. In 2016, Intuit Inc., the company who started Quicken, spun off Quicken, Inc., now a standalone private company. I can't foretell the future, but it's likely the Quicken products will be given a lot more focus by management than when they were just a part of Intuit.

Quicken has several programs from the basic Starter Edition ($40) to their Home & Business product ($120). It's set up to be as easy as tracking things in your checkbook. It also has a mobile app that allows you to snap pictures of your receipts and book them into the system.

If you only have a few business transactions per month, the Starter or Deluxe ($75) editions will suffice. If you're willing to spend a few extra dollars, the Home & Business version separates out your business spending, offers reports on profit/loss projections and cash flow, and alerts you to business deduction options.

## Tax Schedule - Last year  1/1/2015 through 12/31/2015

| Date | Account | Num | Description | Memo | Amount |
|---|---|---|---|---|---|
| − Schedule A | | | | | |
| + Doctors, dentists, hospitals | | | | | -110.00 |
| + Cash charity contributions | | | | | -156.00 |
| | | | | | |
| − Schedule C | | | | | |
| + Gross receipts or sales | | | | | 23,765.00 |
| + Advertising | | | | | -324.56 |
| − Car and truck expenses | | | | | -744.00 |
| 8/8/2015 | Checking | 797 | A1 Auto R... | Bed Liner | -110.00 |
| 9/4/2015 | My Credit Card | ⊕ | Cabot Tire | For Ford | -634.00 |
| + Legal and professional fees | | | | | -827.45 |
| + Office expenses | | | | | -839.00 |
| + Meals and entertainment | | | | | -201.50 |
| + Other business expenses | | | | | -20.00 |

The largest player in the business accounting program market is Intuit, Inc. who makes the large range of QuickBooks products. QuickBooks are geared toward business users, not personal finance, therefore the products have many more features like invoicing, inventory tracking, and robust reporting. They are also more expensive.

One of QuickBooks newer products is their Self-Employed online program. For $10 per month, you download an app to your phone and link it to your bank and credit card accounts. You scan down the charges and deposits and swipe one way if it is personal and the other if it is a business-related transaction.

It allows you to create and send professional looking invoices straight from your phone. The app will track your mileage by using the GPS in your phone. You simply swipe the trip one way if it was personal and the other if it was for business. The system will calculate the business deduction based on current federal rates and record the dollar amount in the system.

It also utilizes the camera to allow you to take a picture of a receipt and notate the business purpose. It will then match the receipt to the credit card charge. At the end of each quarter, QuickBooks Self-Employed calculates your self-employment taxes due. You can even export the data to Intuit's Turbo Tax program.

Self-Employed is a time-saving tool for the entrepreneur who is on the go and is very easy to use. Everything is accessible on your phone and you are able to log in from a desktop computer to see your account. The desktop screen gives you tax checklists, transactions to review, your income to date, and the estimated taxes due.

It doesn't have a full range of reporting options, but makes it easy for you to keep track of deductible expenses and to bill customers on the fly. For the price, it's a convenient and useful tool.

If you have relatively few transactions and don't keep a separate checking account, a Quicken-type or QuickBooks Self-Employed program should be adequate.

A more powerful program is the base desktop product, QuickBooks Pro, which retails for $300. There is also a Premier version that sells for around $500 and includes industry-specific features for contractors, manufacturing, wholesale, professional services, and retail. Unless you need the industry specific features, QuickBooks Pro will probably meet your needs. As your business grows, it's easy to convert the Pro data into the more expensive QuickBooks programs.

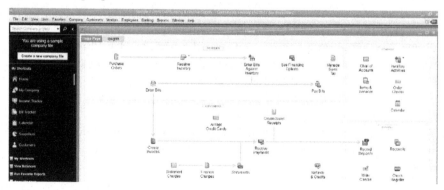

If you need to invoice customers or clients (via email or paper), QuickBooks Pro can handle that as well as track jobs by customer. It's also capable of tracking inventory. The system can download data from your bank and credit card accounts, where you set up rules to have the system automatically record them in the proper accounts.

Because QuickBooks is the industry standard, most e-commerce sites have an option to download your sales data into a format QuickBooks can use. It may require an app with a monthly fee or it may download to a spreadsheet file that you import yourself.

### BANISH Bite # 11

*If you have an e-commerce site, research to see if it will automatically download into an accounting program and if there is an additional cost for this capability.*
*You may wish to choose your accounting program to match.*

There are also several online-based programs to consider. QuickBooks Online (QBO) is available for a base price of $15 per month with various add-ons to take it to $79 per month. As I mentioned earlier in the chapter, an online program is very convenient, but you must be sure your internet access is consistent.

QBO has been improving over the last few years, but it still isn't quite as intuitive as the desktop version, and the reporting is not as robust. Overall, it's a strong program, but if you need job costing, you are better off with the desktop version.

A newer player in the small business accounting field is Xero. They were founded in New Zealand in 2006 with the goal of being the alternative to QuickBooks. They offer only online versions and have almost 900,000 subscribers.

If you are considering an online option, I'd recommend signing up for the free trials and seeing which programs are easiest for you to use. Please be aware that these companies often offer special "Sign up" rates for the first six months and then your price goes up to the regular rate for as long as you use the program. So, when you base your decision on price, make sure you are considering the long-term cost.

Additionally, if you are using an accountant, you may wish to give him or her a call before you decide. Sometimes accountants can offer you a better rate on the same program or can reduce their fees if you are taking some of the time-consuming work off of them. It certainly doesn't hurt to ask.

> ## BANISH Bite #12
>
> *If you use a Mac, you may want to consider a cloud-based system. There are Mac versions of the desktop programs I have listed, but they tend to have less features than the Windows-based versions.*

### D. Automate Where Possible

Whether you choose a spreadsheet, desktop, or online program, you should still try to automate as much of the data entry as possible. Every transaction that is recorded automatically is time you could be growing your business instead. Some of my suggestions will be free options; others are apps and services with a fee. Please look and see which make the most sense for your particular situation.

### 1) Automate entering and paying the bills

Sitting down to pay bills is always a chore. For normal recurring bills, like utilities, car payments, etc., set up the autopay function directly from the vendor. This will pull the money straight from your bank account on a specific date or will charge the amount due to a credit card. You will still need to review these charges, but the autopay saves time and money by not having to handle the paper, write a check, and mail it or use the electronic check option each month. Quicken Home and Business will also automate this for you.

> ## BANISH Bite # 13
>
> *Be sure your checking account keeps a large enough balance to handle any automatic withdrawals. The value of the time savings can easily be wiped out with overdraft fees.*

Many banks offer a free or low-cost bill paying option. Simply log into your online bank account, set up the vendor to pay, and have the bank mail a physical check or draft your account. If you're using an accounting program that pulls in your bank data, you establish the rules to code the bills to the correct expense account.

Once you have more transactions than you want to key in and are willing to pay a bit more, check out Bill.com. You scan, fax, email, and/or have the vendors email the bills directly to Bill.com. They sort them and send you back an email with the backup to approve payment. You or your designated person approves (or disapproves) the payments, and Bill.com mails the checks or pays them electronically for you. It will also sync the transactions with your QuickBooks, QBO, or Xero accounting system.

The nice part of Bill.com is the ability to be anywhere and still make sure the bills are paid on time without having to do any data entry. This is another product to ask your accountant about for cost savings.

### 2) Match the Credit Card Charges and Receipts

If you're like me, you pay with your credit card more than with checks or being sent invoices. See if your credit card company has an app that will allow you to take a picture of your receipts and match them to the charges as they come through. This is a great way to make certain you have the documentation you need. It's also very helpful when there is a charge for something and the vendor name is one you don't recognize. If the system has matched the receipt, you've got your answer right away. If not, you know you need to investigate.

Even if you aren't using a dedicated program to match the snapshot of the receipts to your accounts, you can use your phone and save it to a file on a Google Drive or Dropbox type account. Get in the habit of doing that and you'll be amazed how much easier pulling together the information is.

### 3) Streamline Invoicing Your Customers

We all like to get money coming in, but sometimes we have to ask for it. If you have customers that need invoices on a recurring basis, investing in a good accounting system will help. Programs like QuickBooks, QBO, and Xero allow you to set up recurring invoices that can automatically go out on a certain day of the month. You can also set up merchant accounts so the customer can click on a link in the emailed invoice to pay the bill directly out of their bank account. Bill.com, Quicken Home and Business, and QuickBooks Self-Employed also has good invoicing options.

Here is an example from QuickBooks Pro on setting up a recurring invoice.

You can set it to automatically generate an invoice or simply be added to a reminder list for you to review and manually send. The **How Often** box allows you to select various options from daily to annually.

### 4) Don't forget to link the bank and credit card accounts

With as many of your payments and receipts automated as possible, you'll spend a lot less time having to manually key in data. Next, be sure to link your credit card and bank accounts to your accounting system, so every charge or deposit is also included.

As you review the data that has been downloaded, you will be matching it to the receipts and payments already loaded. Reconciling your accounts is then so much easier than manually checking off items on your bank statement.

### BANISH Action Steps

- *Decide if you need and can afford a full accounting system, a simplified app-based system, or if a spreadsheet will do.*

- *Evaluate online versus desktop options and determine which will work best for you.*

- *Request free trials of any accounting package you are considering and play around with their sample companies.*

- *Look for every way possible to automate your data entry within your budget constraints.*

*Ozzie and Harriet Nelson successfully argued that they could deduct the clothes worn on the TV series. Even though the clothes were of the current fashion, they were kept at the studio and never worn outside and therefore considered deductible.*

## BANISH Step 4—Import Your Transactions

You've decided the type of system to use, and now it is time to start recording your data. It's crucial that you designate a time to do your bookkeeping each week, or every two weeks, and stick to that time slot. It doesn't matter when—pick a few hours that work best for you. If you have a full-time job outside your business, the time may be Saturday morning before the kids get up or late Wednesday night. Believe it or not, keeping to a set schedule will save you more time than most anything else.

In case you're wondering why I believe this, let me share some examples.

I was working with a church whose bookkeeping hours kept creeping up. When I asked why, the bookkeeper explained that he couldn't leave at his designated time because people kept coming in with last minute requests.

My immediate and seemingly heartless response was, "Why didn't you tell them to come back next week?"

"I can't do that. They need their money."

At this point, it was an education process. Yes, the volunteers and vendors need to be paid, but their decision to wait until the last minute was costing the church. I insisted he inform everyone that checks were only going to be cut on Tuesdays, and they had to be approved by the pastor on Monday before they would be paid on Tuesday.

"It will never work!" the bookkeeper moaned.

"You'll get lots of complaints for two weeks, but then they will be trained," I assured him.

The poor bookkeeper was miserable for the two weeks, but by the third week, everyone had their check requests in on Monday and his hours went down dramatically.

You may be thinking, "But my business is just me, I don't have those kinds of distractions." Well, let's step through a typical day.

It's Saturday morning and you realize you have a stack of bills and emails to get through. You sit at your computer and start to write checks. Then one of your chat apps dings. It's your sister who saw you were online and messaged you with a fun emoticon. You respond in kind and then go back to the stack of bills.

Had you already paid that one? Or was it the one you were going to do next? So, you dig through the checks you had written and found you had already paid it. Just as you are reviewing the next stack of paperwork, the dogs bark. Realizing you hadn't fed them yet, you get up to do that.

Now back at your desk, you decide to look through the emails for bills that need to be paid. Oh, there is an ad for those cute shoes (or fancy gadget, or whatever) you've been wanting. Suddenly you're surfing the internet.

Better check Facebook while you are here—you never know what new cat video is up.

Two hours have suddenly gone by, and you don't have your basic bookkeeping done. Where did the day go?

### BANISH Bite #14

*Set up a designated time to do your bookkeeping and shut the door, turn off your phone, turn off all notifications, and close any browsers you don't need.*

*If you get tempted to look at social media, promise yourself you will schedule it in later in the day as your reward for finishing the bookkeeping.*

Every time you are distracted from a task, it takes time to get back to your project. This is time that could have been spent growing your business instead. So be disciplined and make the people around you understand how important it is for you to focus.

### A. Design a Chart of Accounts for Your Business

In the last chapter, I asked you to research and decide what type of accounting system would work best for you. Whether you're using a simple spreadsheet or a robust online system, you will be using a **Chart of Accounts**.

The chart of accounts is a list of account names and numbers that you will post transactions into. They are divided into Asset accounts (remember—things you own), Liabilities (things you owe), Equity (what's left over for you), Income (sales—yeah!), Cost of Goods Sold (the cost of the items sold), and Expenses (all the other costs).

You'll want account names that mean something to you. For example, call your checking account **1000 Checking** or if you have two checking accounts, you may prefer **1001 First Bank Checking** and **1002 Fidelity Checking**.

For the numbering sequence, I recommend:

1000-1999—Asset (checking, accounts receivable, equipment, etc.)

2000-2999—Liability (accounts payable, bank loan, customer deposits)

3000-3999—Equity (probably only need one for now)

4000-4999—Income (website sales, wholesale sales, retail sales, etc.)

5000-5999—COGS (production/purchase costs—only need if you sell physical products)

6000-7999—Expenses (all other costs to run your business).

Now look at the reports we pulled together in the first chapter. At a minimum, you will need accounts for the bank account, an equity account, and all the lines on the IRS Form 1040 Schedule C your business may use.

For example, on the spreadsheet I designed shown on the next page, my chart of accounts mirrors the expenses on Schedule C, even to numbering them based on the tax return line item. Past expense number 6027, I would include types of items not specifically addressed above.

If you're using a more complex accounting system with a range of reporting capabilities, your chart of accounts should be designed to group like expenses together, i.e. all your promotional and marketing expenses would go to accounts 6300-6399, and your office and administrative expenses would go in accounts 6400-6499. Even with a stronger accounting system, I like to keep the number of specific accounts to a minimum. If you have too many accounts, you are less likely to code the bills consistently.

Many accounting programs offer a suggested chart of accounts. Look over any suggested for you, but I'll warn you they are usually far more detailed than you need. Simply set up the basics as I've mentioned here, or, if you are using QuickBooks, check out www.AccountantBesideYou.com, where I'll be offering charts of accounts for various types of small businesses and the instructions to easily import them into your system.

Look at the other reports you need. Does the bank want expenses classified in certain ways? Do you need to differentiate different business units?

For example, on my e-commerce site, I sell resources for religious organizations, nonprofits, and small businesses. My accounting system sets each of these up as a business unit (or a Class as it is called in QuickBooks) so I can run reports on each individually or combined.

Perhaps you have an eBay store and are also an Amazon Affiliate. You probably want to track the revenue and expenses for each so you know how to focus your time. Maybe you have a couple of unrelated businesses, i.e. you are an Uber driver and sell Pampered Chef. Though they can be combined on

Schedule C for the IRS, you'll want the ability to see the financial results separately.

## My Business

### 2016

### Chart of Accounts

| Account Number | Account Description |
|---|---|
| | **Revenue** |
| 4001 | Income 1 |
| 4002 | Income 2 |
| 4003 | Income 3 |
| 4004 | Income 4 |
| 4005 | Income 5 |
| 4006 | Income 6 |
| 4007 | Returns and Allowances |
| 4008 | Other Income |
| 5001 | Cost of Goods Sold type 2 |
| 5002 | Cost of Goods Sold type 3 |
| | **EXPENSES** |
| 6008 | Advertising |
| 6009 | Car and Truck Expenses |
| 6010 | Commission and Fees |
| 6011 | Contract Labor |
| 6012 | Depletion |
| 6013 | Depreciation and Section 179 |
| 6014 | Employee Benefit Programs |
| 6015 | Insurance |
| 6016-a | Interest-Mortgage |
| 6016-b | Interest-Other |
| 6017 | Legal and Professional Services |
| 6018 | Office Expense |
| 6019 | Pension and Profit-Sharing Plans |
| 6020-a | Rent/Lease-Vehicle |

COA | BTA | Summary by Month | GL-Jan | Jan | GL-Feb |

Once you have your chart of accounts set, it's time to automate the data we discussed in the last chapter.

## B. Record Transactions—The Basics

I'll show you specifics on recording different types of income and expenses, but first I want you to understand some accounting basics.

We accountants love the double-entry accounting. This simply means every transaction has two sides—*debits* and *credits*. They are not good or bad; they are simply opposite sides of an equation.

A check register uses a double-entry system even if you didn't realize it. Cash deposited from a sale increased the cash (debited) and increased the revenues (credited) by the same amount, but a roll of stamps purchased decreased cash (credited) and increased expenses (debited) by the same amount.

Debits and credits affect each type of account, assets, liabilities, equity, income, and expense in a particular way.

## Impact of Debits & Credits on Account Types

| Account | Debit | Credit |
|---|---|---|
| **Assets** | Increases | Decreases |
| **Liabilities** | Decreases | Increases |
| **Equity** | Decreases | Increases |
| **Income** | Decreases | Increases |
| **Expense** | Increases | Decreases |

For example, *Cash* is an asset. Any increases to cash will be recorded as a debit and any decreases as a credit. If we receive money, we debit cash (because it increased) and need to credit another account, *Revenue*.

Revenue is an income account, and, from the chart above, we see that we need to credit it to increase the income.

If you were to write this out as a journal entry, it would look like this:

| | Debit | Credit |
|---|---|---|
| Cash | $100.00 | |
| Sales | | $100.00 |

The total amount of the debits **must** equal the credits.

Don't worry if you feel your eyes glazing over at this point. The good news is most accounting programs do the two sides of the entry for you. You rarely need to record actual journal entries.

We'll start by focusing on paying the bills, and then I'll step you through recording your income.

## C. What is Deductible?

It's important to understand what is deductible for IRS purposes to capture every expense necessary. As we discussed in the previous chapter, your chart of accounts should be set up around the expense lines on the Schedule C. For easy reference, I have listed each of these lines in the Appendix and explained what types of expenditures is allowed.

### BANISH Bite #15
*The primary rule of whether an expense is deductible for tax purpose is:*

*Is it **necessary** and is it **reasonable**?*

*It may be necessary to have a way to keep time in your office, but it is not reasonable for it to be a Rolex.*

You may also have deductible non-business expenses (mortgage interest, property taxes, charitable contributions, medical, tuition, child care, etc.). In your chart of accounts list, add these with similar account numbers. For example, all personal deductible expenses would start with 8xxx (8010 Mortgage Interest, 8020 Child Care, etc.). That way when you run reports, everything is grouped together and you can easily back out the personal items when calculating the business expenses.

Non-deductible expenses also must be recorded to make your bank balance. I suggest you set up accounts together in the 9xxx series if you don't have a separate business account. If you do, any personal expenses accidentally paid from there should be considered Shareholder Distributions, an equity account (3xxx series).

### D. Paying the Bills

No matter what accounting system you choose, automate your bills wherever possible. In the last chapter, I explained how to utilize the automatic online pay options for your normal recurring bills like telephone, web hosting, etc. as long as you are careful to keep an adequate cash balance in your bank account. You can link programs like Quicken Home and Business to your online bills and have the system automatically show the upcoming charge and generate the payment, so you'll know if there will be enough cash when the payment is made.

## 1) Using a spreadsheet

If you have few expenses and are using a spreadsheet for your system, you will record your checks in your spreadsheet. If you're using the one from the www.AccountantBesideYou.com website or similar, you'll enter your beginning bank balance at the top of January's General Ledger tab.

### MY BUSINESS
### GENERAL LEDGER
### JANUARY

| Date | Item Description | Ck# | Etsy Store | | Balance |
|---|---|---|---|---|---|
| | | | Debit (Expenses) | Credit (Income) | |
| 4001 | **INCOME 1** | | | | |
| | Beginning Balance | | | $ 1,000.00 | 1,000.00 |
| | Total | | 0.00 | 0.00 | |
| **Expenses:** | | | | | |
| 6008 | **ADVERTISING** | | | | |
| 1/20/18 | Facebook ad | cc1-18 | 50.00 | | 950.00 |
| | | | | | 950.00 |
| | Total | | 0.00 | 0.00 | |
| 6009 | **CAR AND TRUCK EXPENSES** | | | | |
| | | | | | 950.00 |
| | | | | | 950.00 |
| | Total | | 0.00 | 0.00 | |
| 6010 | **COMMISSION AND FEES** | | | | |
| | | | | | 950.00 |
| | | | | | 950.00 |
| | | | | | 950.00 |
| | Total | | 0.00 | 0.00 | |
| 6011 | **CONTRACT LABOR** | | | | |
| 1/15/18 | Betsy Smith-Website design | 1001 | 500.00 | | 450.00 |
| | | | | | 450.00 |
| | | | | | 450.00 |
| | Total | | 500.00 | 0.00 | |
| | **Monthly beginning total** | | | 1000.00 | |
| | **Total debits (expenses)** | | 550.00 | | 550.00 |
| | **Total credits (income)** | | | 0.00 | 0.00 |
| | **Monthly End Total** | | | 450.00 | $ 450.00 |

*(Annotations overlaid on image: Beginning cash balance, Credit card charge, Check paid, Ending cash balance)*

| INTRO | Directory | COA | BTA | Summary by Month | GL-Jan | Jan | GL-Feb |

Next, let's assume you paid Betsy Smith $500 for some design work for your website. You would record it under the Contract Labor expense, noting the related check number. If you also paid the credit card bill of $50 for Facebook ads, you would record it under Advertising with a notation of which credit card bill it was from.

If you have several credit card charges on the bill, the expenses must add up to the total amount of the bill paid for the bank balance to be correct.

Now the spreadsheet shows you started out with $1000 and paid $550 of expenses ($500 for website plus $50 for ads), leaving you with an ending balance of $450. You'll want to enter these in the spreadsheet every time you write checks (during your designated bookkeeping time we discussed earlier). Don't forget to input the recurring bills that are automatically drafted out of your account. If the amount is always the same, go ahead and input those into future months.

### 2) Using a computerized accounting system

If you're using a computerized accounting system, you'll have already set up your chart of accounts as we discussed in the last chapter and linked your bank and credit cards to the system.

This is where the automation comes in handy. If you're using a mobile app like QuickBooks Self-Employed, you refresh the screen and a list of new charges to your bank or credit card appears. Scan through them, swipe right if it's personal, swipe left if it's a business expense.

The left swipe will ask you what account to put the charge in. If you are unsure, refer to the Appendix or leave it in Uncategorized to come back to later.

If you have a receipt, use the Attach Receipt feature to take a picture of it. That way you have your receipts tied directly to your expenditures.

If you are working on your computer rather than the phone, it's easy to set up rules, so every time you have a charge from a specific vendor, the system moves the expense to the designated category.

Suppose you pay cash for an item that is a deductible expense. QuickBooks Self-Employed allows you to add it on the go by selecting the plus sign in the top right corner. Explain the business purpose, code it to the correct account, and add the receipt. Now there is no excuse not to catch every available deduction.

For products like Quicken Home and Business, enter bill payments directly into the check register. You can designate the check number if you manually wrote the check, or print it later.

Be sure to use the **Payee** name, a memo to explain why it is deductible, and select the category (i.e. the account from the chart of accounts). The system offers a default chart of accounts under the **Business** category that mirrors the expenses on the Schedule C.

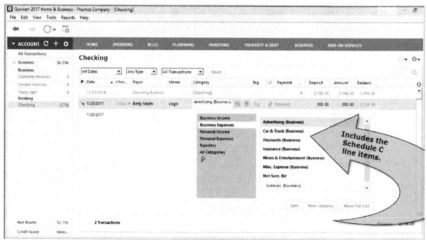

If you use the **Business** tab at the top, select *Business Actions, Bills and vendors, Create bill.*

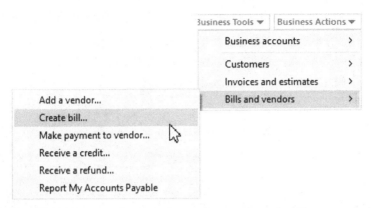

This will bring up a form to input the purchase in. You can tie it to a customer or job and tag it for further classification.

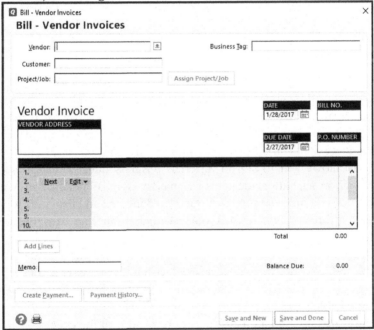

Once saved, Quicken will display the amount as an upcoming expense to track your expected cash flow.

The more expensive programs also do this and allow more categorization. Here is an example from QuickBooks.

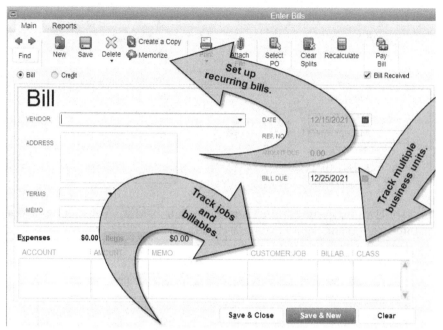

You enter the vendor name and amount due and code it to the correct expense account. There are options to track whether this expense is related to and billable to a particular customer and/or job, which is useful for project and construction work. The other useful option is CLASS.

Class allows you to set up different business units or categories. For example, if you sell handmade items via an eBay store, as an Amazon Affiliate, and on Etsy, you may want to track the related income and expenses for each. If so, set up three separate classes: one called eBay, another Amazon, and the third, Etsy.

Other examples of using classes include: if you sell crafts made by other people as well as yourself, you may instead wish to have classes associated with each person; or if you have several different Airbnb locations, you could use a different class for each.

Once the bills are entered, you can print and mail the checks. When you download your bank transactions, the system will attempt to automatically match the transactions to your entries.

In the example above, the system tied eight of the manually-entered transactions into the information downloaded from the bank. It also recognized for one transaction that a RULE had previously been established, leaving only one transaction for you to specify the account.

Please note, the system has not recorded these transactions yet. This screen gives you the opportunity to change any of the accounts. Once you are satisfied, you will ADD/APPROVE to record them in the system.

Though the above screen is from a QuickBooks desktop program, other accounting programs and the online versions will have similar options.

### E. Recording Your Income

How are you paid? Do your customers buy directly from you and pay cash? Do they buy online via PayPal or credit cards and the money deposited automatically in your checking account a few days later? Or do you invoice customers and wait for checks? Next, I'll go over some of the usual ways of recording sales.

### 1) Recording service or consulting income

Let's assume you are a graphic artist who freelances. You contracted with a client who agreed to pay you $300 for a new logo. When you complete the work, you email them an invoice asking for the $300. A week later, they mail you the check.

If you're using a spreadsheet or other basic system, after you receive the check and deposit the cash in the bank, you would record the $300 to a 4xxx Consulting Income account.

If you're using a mobile app like QB Self-Employed, a convenient feature is the ability to invoice directly from your phone while you are at the client's location or anywhere you have internet service.

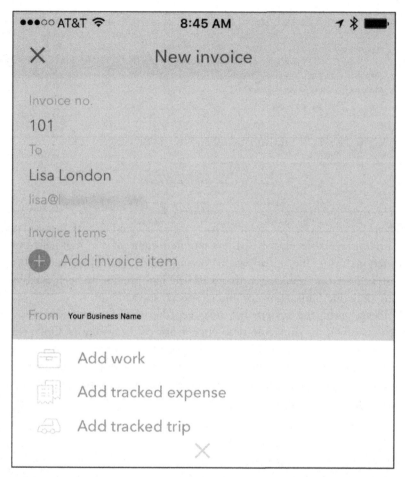

This app pulls customer information from your phone contact list and allows you to add any description and price under the **Add work** option. It will also remember the type of work you're adding so you don't have to rekey it every time. Additionally, if you have an expense or mileage that should be charged to the client, select it directly from the system to have it included on the invoice.

I added mileage to the client, and the invoice looks the one on the next page.

If you sign up for Intuit's (the company who makes QuickBooks) credit card services, include a link on the invoice for the client to pay the invoice directly. This is a handy feature for your client as well as a way for you to get the money quicker.

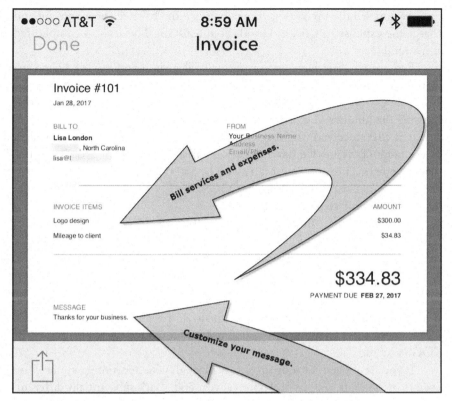

In a computerized accounting system, you would input the sale into a customer invoice which would be recorded as an Accounts Receivable (most will let you email it directly from the computer), and designate it as 4xxx Consulting Income. This allows you to keep track of the money that is owed to you. When you receive the check, you would apply it to the customer account in the Accounts Receivable section, and the system would record it into the designated bank account.

### 2) Record cash at the time of the sale

If you didn't need to invoice your customer, you would enter the money received in the bank account and the same amount in your income (Sales 4xxx) account. Many systems refer to this as a **Sales Receipt** (not a **Sales Invoice** as discussed above).

### 3) Sales of inventory

When you purchase merchandise to sale or to be used in the production of an item, it is not directly expensed, but recorded in an **Inventory** account. This is an asset on the balance sheet because you own it.

As you sell the inventory, you will reduce the balance sheet amount and charge the expense to Cost of Goods Sold (COGS). This isn't as complicated as it sounds.

Perhaps you buy earrings from a small village in Honduras for $2 and sell them to stores locally for $5. When you drop off 20 earrings, the store gives you a check for the wholesale value of $100. You give them a sales receipt showing the number of earrings and the total transaction.

The $100 received will be recorded both as a sale (4xxx) and as deposited to the bank (1xxx) as we have discussed earlier. Additionally, you'll need to reduce your Inventory account (an asset) by $40 ($2 x the 20 sold) and charge the expense to Cost of Goods Sold (COGS).

Your income statement will show:

| | |
|---|---|
| Income | $100 |
| COGS | (40) |
| Net Income | $ 60 |

If your accounting system tracks inventory, it will also allow you to set up your products to automatically record the cost of goods sold at the time of the sale. If not, the adjustments can be made manually at the end of the month or year. Unless you had a theft, the adjustment amount should be recorded in the COGS account.

If you have been tracking inventory through your accounting system, you need to reconcile it to a physical count at year end. If it's substantially different, research whether it was set up in the system incorrectly or if you've experienced theft or loss. Either way, your accounting system should match the physical count.

In Step 5, I'll show you how to use the tax forms to calculate your cost of goods sold.

### BANISH Bite #16

*At the end of the year, always count the inventory you have left. Multiply it by the COST of the products (not how much you sell it for). This is your ending inventory value and will be the beginning of the year inventory value for the next year's tax return.*

### 4) Payments from E-commerce and/or websites

Perhaps you are an Amazon Affiliate. Your revenues are handled through the company website, and they pay your checking account directly on a periodic basis (monthly). It is simplest to record the total sale for the period as one amount. Record the sale in the designated income account (i.e. Amazon Affiliate Sales 4xxx) and in the checking account when it is posted.

If the amount transferred into your account usually has a corporate fee already deducted, i.e. the company may take its commission before transferring the cash, record the amount received as your income amount. This will be important when reconciling your year-end information later.

If the company gives you detailed information, you may wish to record transactions by date to understand which days of the week are your best revenue producer or by customer if you have access to their emails to run promotions directly to them. This may require you to enter the data manually or upload through a spreadsheet program.

Applications are often developed for popular programs that will automatically import the data for you. Depending on the app and the accounting software you're using, there may be a monthly cost. For example, if you have an Etsy store or are an Uber driver, check out QuickBooks Self-Employed. Intuit (the company who makes QuickBooks) has partnered with each of these companies to have instant integration of the sales with the accounting program.

### 5) Payments from PayPal and credit cards

This can sometimes get a little complicated. Your credit card company charges you a discount fee for each sales transaction. Often this is a combination of a percentage amount plus a per transaction fee. For example, if you use Square, they currently charge 2.75% per swipe (or dip or tap) and 3.5% plus 15 cents per keyed-in transaction.

Some companies deposit the full amount of the daily sales into your bank account as they occur (usually with a 2-3 day settlement window) and then once a month, charge you the discount fee. If your company does this, you are lucky. It's the easiest way to track the sales and the fees.

In this situation, you record the daily sales as discussed earlier in the chapter and simply treat the discount fee as part of COGS when it hits your bank.

Square, PayPal, and other popular payment processors take the discount before they deposit the money in your bank. This means if you have a $40 sale, your bank deposit will show $38.90 ($40-$1.10 fee). The most technically correct way to record this is to show the $40 sale and the $1.10 in the COGS. But if you automated your bank account to record deposits automatically into your system, this means you would have to manually adjust each day's deposit to increase the sales and move the dollars into COGS. I'd suggest treating the net amount as the sale so it matches the daily deposits. Your gross income will still be correct for tax purposes.

### 6) Bartering

Bartering is the trading of goods or services without exchanging money. It can be a very convenient way to pay for business services without affecting your cash flow. Just be aware that the value of the bartered good must be recorded as income. For example, if you are a graphic artist and traded a design of a logo in exchange for an accountant to prepare your tax return, you would record the value of the logo design as income (a credit) and an equal amount to professional services expense (a debit). It is crucial you keep a paper trail of the barter!

If you bartered a product for a non-business item, you still must record the income. Instead of an expense, you will charge the amount to Shareholder Distributions (an equity account which we will discuss next).

## F.  Paying Yourself

As a self-employed business owner, you will not pay yourself as an employee. Instead, the government will charge you income and payroll taxes on the net income (sales less deductible expenses) of your business.

> *Any money given to the owner in a sole proprietorship is considered a **Draw**, not an expense. This means the owner is drawing part of the business earnings out of the business.*
>
> *You will be charged taxes on the net income of the business, not the total amount of the draws.*

Assuming you have a separate checking account for your business, you may wish to pay a regular draw.  Your draw account will be an **Equity** account (3xxx), not an expense account. The check would be made out to you, and the expenditure recorded in the 3xxx Draw account. Any personal expenditures accidentally charged to the business credit card or paid out of the business account would also go to this account.

If your business money is being run through your personal checking account, you don't need to set up a draw account.

Even if you don't take any money out of the business account, you are still required to pay self-employment (SE) and income taxes. The SE tax consists of both the employer and employee portions of Social Security and Medicare taxes.

This means you need to pay estimated taxes on a quarterly basis and file an annual return if you expect to owe $1000 or more in taxes from your self-employment income. Please check www.irs.gov for current earnings levels.

Over the next several pages, I'll step you through the process of calculating the self-employment tax and how to make the quarterly payments. First go to www.irs.gov and search for Publication 505 and Form 1040-ES. Download the PDFs to your computer for ease of use.

**Publication 505 Tax Withholding and Estimated Tax** explains tax withholding and estimated taxes for all different types of income, not just your sole proprietorship. It's a great reference for questions about taxable fringe benefits, who must pay estimated taxes, and what the penalties are. Form 1040-ES is where you will calculate your estimated taxes.

Next find your last year's tax return. You will reference it for several of the calculations. To start your estimation, look to see how much money your business made after expenses last year. If this is your first year, estimate what you think it will make based on the information you have thus far.

On page 6 of **Form 1040-ES**, you will find the following form. I'm going to fill it out with you, using very basic assumptions.

**2017 Self-Employment Tax and Deduction Worksheet for Lines 1 and 11 of the Estimated Tax Worksheet**                          Keep for *Your Records*

*Expected profit for the year.*

1a. Enter your expected income and profits subject to self-employment tax* ......... 1a. _12,000_

If you will have farm income and also receive social security retirement or disability *This is the Medicare portion of the tax.* enter your expected Conservation Reserve Program payments that will be ... on Schedule F (Form 1040) or listed on Schedule K-1 (Form 1065) ..... b. _∅_

2. ... 1b from line 1a ............................................. 2. _12,000_
3. ... by 92.35% (0.9235) ....................................... 3. _11,082_
   ... line 3 by 2.9% (0.029) .................................. 4. _321_
5. Social security tax maximum income ............................ 5. $127,200
6. Enter your expected wages (if subject to social security tax or the 6.2% portion of tier 1 railroad retirement tax) ............................ 6. _50,000_   *From your jobs that give you a paycheck.*
7. Subtract line 6 from line 5 .................................. 7. _77,200_
   Note. *If line 7 is zero or less, enter -0- on line 9 and skip to line 10.*
8. Enter the **smaller** of line 3 or line 7 ...................... 8. _11,082_
9. Multiply line 8 by 12.4% (0.124) ............................. 9. _1374_
10. Add lines 4 and 9. Enter the result here and on line 11 of your 2017 Estimated Tax Worksheet ......... 10. _1695_
11. Multiply line 10 by 50% (0.50). This is your expected deduction for self-employment tax on Form 1040, line 27. Subtract this amount when figuring your expected AGI on line 1 of your 2017 Estimated Tax Worksheet ............... 11. _848_

* Your net profit from self-employment is found on Schedule C (Form 1040), line 31; Schedule F (Form 1040), line 34; Schedule K-1 (Form 1065), box 14, code A; and Schedule K-1 (Form 1065-B), box 9, code J1.

On **Line 1a** enter your expected net income from your sole proprietorship. If you have several businesses, you'll need to add them together for this line. This is an estimate, not actual net income, so you'll want to base it on last year's results and any expected changes.

For example, if last year you had $12,000 in net income from sales of craft items on your website, but the site was only up for six months of the year, you need to raise your expected net income for this year. If, however, your product was one that only sells at Christmas time, you may not want to increase this estimate.

The next line relates to farm income and Social Security benefits. Sorry, but that is beyond the scope of our discussion, so we'll leave it blank.

**Line 3** reduces your income by 7.65% (the combined rate of SS and Medicare rates). The amount on Line 3 is then multiplied by 2.9% to calculate the Medicare tax for **Line 4**.

> *The 2017 tax rate for Medicare is 1.45 % for the employer and 1.45% for the employee. The Social Security rate is 6.2% for the employer and 6.2% for the employee.*
>
> *As a self-employed individual, you are both the employer and employee, so you owe 2.9% (1.45 x 2) for Medicare and 12.4% (6.2 x 2) for Social Security for a total of 15.3%.*

Social security has a maximum income level which is shown on **Line 5**. For **Line 6**, you'll put in your expected wages (that someone else will withhold employment taxes on). In this example, you are making $50,000 at a job that gives you a regular paycheck. This is $77,200 less than the Social Security limit (**Line 7**), so enter your small business income from Line 3 onto Line 8.

**Line 8** is multiplied by 12.4% (the employer and employee share of Social Security tax for the amount on **Line 9**.

Add lines 4 and 9 to get the total of the estimated self-employment tax for your business on **Line 10**. **Line 11** calculates the deductible portion of that amount. This is the equivalent of the employer's share of SE taxes.

Now what? This gives us the data we need to fill out the **Estimated Tax Worksheet** as shown on the next page.

Starting at the top, **Line 1,** adjusted gross income should be the total of your wages and the net income from your business. (Other income also goes there, but for purposes of this book, I'm assuming you only have these two sources.) Using the example above, wages were $50,000 and net income from the business was $12,000. Reduce the total by $848 for the deductible part of the self-employment tax (Line 11 above) for approximately $61,000.

**2017 Estimated Tax Worksheet** — Keep for Your Records

| | | | |
|---|---|---|---|
| 1 | Adjusted gross income you expect in 2017 (see instructions) . | 1 | 61,000 |
| 2 | • If you plan to itemize deductions, enter the estimated total of your itemized deductions. | | |
| | **Caution:** *If line 1 is over $156,900 your deduction may be reduced. See Pub. 505 for details.* | | |
| | • If you do not plan to itemize deductions, enter your standard deduction. | 2 | 6,000 |
| 3 | Subtract line 2 from line 1. . . . . . . . . . . . . . . . . . . . | 3 | 55,000 |
| 4 | Exemptions. Multiply $4,050 by the number of personal exemptions. **Caution:** *See Worksheet 2-6 in Pub. 505 to figure the amount to enter if line 1 is over: $156,900* . . . . . . . . . . . . . | 4 | (4,050) |
| 5 | Subtract line 4 from line 3 . . . . . . . . . . . . . . . . . . | 5 | 50,950 |
| 6 | Tax. Figure your tax on the amount on line 5 by using the **2017 Tax Rate Schedules**. | | |
| | **Caution:** *If you will have qualified dividends or a net capital gain, or expect to exclude or deduct foreign earned income or housing, see Worksheets 2-7 and 2-8 in Pub. 505 to figure the tax.* . . . | 6 | 7,901 |
| 7 | Alternative minimum tax from **Form 6251** or included on **Form 1040A, line 28** . . . . . | 7 | |
| 8 | Add lines 6 and 7. Add to this amount any other taxes you expect to include in the total on Form 1040, line 44 . . . . . . . . . . . . . . . . . . . . . . . . . . . . . . | 8 | 7,901 |
| 9 | Credits (see instructions). **Do not** include any income tax withholding on this line . . . . . . | 9 | |
| 10 | Subtract line 9 from line 8. If zero or less, enter -0- . . . . . . . . . . . . . . . | 10 | 7,901 |
| 11 | Self-employment tax (see instructions) . . . . . . . . . . . . . . . . . . . | 11 | 1,695 |
| 12 | Other taxes (see instructions) . . . . . . . . . . . . . . . . . . . . . | 12 | |
| 13a | Add lines 10 through 12 . . . . . . . . . . . . . . . . . . . . . . . | 13a | 9,596 |
| b | Earned income credit, additional child tax credit, fuel tax credit, net premium tax credit, refundable American opportunity credit, and refundable credit from Form 8885 . . . . . . . | 13b | |
| c | **Total 2017 estimated tax.** Subtract line 13b from line 13a. If zero or less, enter -0- . . . ▶ | 13c | 9,596 |
| 14a | Multiply line 13c by 90% (66²/₃% for farmers and fishermen) . . . . | 14a | 8,636 | |
| b | Required annual payment based on prior year's tax (see instructions) . | 14b | 8,000 | |
| c | **Required annual payment to avoid a penalty.** Enter the **smaller** of line 14a or 14b . . . ▶ | 14c | 8,000 |
| | **Caution:** *Generally, if you do not prepay (through income tax withholding and estimated tax payments) at least the amount on line 14c, you may owe a penalty for not paying enough estimated tax. To avoid a penalty, make sure your estimate on line 13c is as accurate as possible. Even if you pay the required annual payment, you may still owe tax when you file your return. If you prefer, you can pay the amount shown on line 13c. For details, see chapter 2 of Pub. 505.* | | |
| 15 | Income tax withheld and estimated to be withheld during 2017 (including income tax withholding on pensions, annuities, certain deferred income, etc.) . . . . . . . . . . | 15 | 4600 |
| 16a | Subtract line 15 from line 14c . . . . . . . . . . . . . . . . | 16a | 3400 |
| | Is the result zero or less? | | |
| | ☐ **Yes. Stop here.** You are not required to make estimated tax payments. | | |
| | ☑ **No.** Go to line 16b. | | |
| b | Subtract line 15 from line 13c . . . . . . . . . . . . . . . . | 16b | 4996 |
| | Is the result less than $1,000? | | |
| | ☐ **Yes. Stop here.** You are not required to make estimated tax payments. | | |
| | ☑ **No.** Go to line 17 to figure your required payment. | | |
| 17 | If the first payment you are required to make is due April 18, 2017, enter ¼ of line 16a (minus any 2016 overpayment that you are applying to this installment) here, and on your estimated tax payment voucher(s) if you are paying by check or money order . . . . . . . . | 17 | 850 |

**Line 2** is where you estimate your deductions (if you aren't taking the standard deduction). I've put $6000 in for my example. **Line 3** simply deducts Line 2 from Line 1. **Line 4** is the standard exemption. This is the number of exemptions you use for your regular tax return (based on your marital situation, number of dependents, etc.). The exemptions are subtracted to give you the taxable income on **Line 5**.

For **Line 6**, you will calculate the expected tax using the tax rate schedules found at www.irs.gov/pub/irs-pdf/n1036.pdf.

TABLE 7—ANNUAL Payroll Period

| (a) SINGLE person (including head of household)— | | | (b) MARRIED person— | | |
|---|---|---|---|---|---|
| If the amount of wages (after subtracting withholding allowances) is: | | The amount of income tax to withhold is: | If the amount of wages (after subtracting withholding allowances) is: | | The amount of income tax to withhold is: |
| Not over $2,300 . . . . . . . | | $0 | Not over $8,650 . . . . . . . | | $0 |
| Over— | But not over— | of excess over— | Over— | But not over— | of excess over— |
| $2,300 | —$11,625 | $0.00 plus 10% . . . —$2,300 | $8,650 | —$27,300 | $0.00 plus 10% . . . —$8,650 |
| $11,625 | —$40,250 | $932.50 plus 15% . . . —$11,625 | $27,300 | —$84,550 | $1,865.00 plus 15% . . . —$27,300 |
| $40,250 | —$94,200 | $5,226.25 plus 25% . . . —$40,250 | $84,550 | —$161,750 | $10,452.50 plus 25% . . . —$84,550 |
| $94,200 | —$193,950 | $18,713.75 plus 28% . . . —$94,200 | $161,750 | —$242,000 | $29,752.50 plus 28% . . . —$161,750 |
| $193,950 | —$419,000 | $46,643.75 plus 33% . . . —$193,950 | $242,000 | —$425,350 | $52,222.50 plus 33% . . . —$242,000 |
| $419,000 | —$420,700 | $120,910.25 plus 35% . . . —$419,000 | $425,350 | —$479,350 | $112,728.00 plus 35% . . . —$425,350 |
| $420,700 | | $121,505.25 plus 39.6% . . . —$420,700 | $479,350 | | $131,628.00 plus 39.6% . . . —$479,350 |

To use the tax rates table, first find the table labeled ANNUAL Payroll Period. Next, find the column with your filing status (Single, Married, Head of Household, etc.). Look down the column until you see the taxable income range where the number in Line 5 falls. It will give you the base tax amount for that range. Next, subtract the $40,250 from your taxable income number. This is the incremental amount that will be multiplied by the percentage listed in the column.

| | |
|---|---|
| Tax on Base on $50,950 | $5,226 |
| Incremental Taxable Income ($50,950 less $40,250=$10,700) | |
| Tax on Incremental at 25% (.25 * $10,700) | 2,675 |
| Total Tax due per tax rate schedule | $7,901 |

**Lines 7-9** address alternate minimum tax and credits which we won't worry about for this example.

**Line 10** will equal Line 6 (because we didn't have anything in 7-9).

**Line 11** shows the $1695 from the self-employment tax calculations we did a few pages back.

**Line 12** will include other taxes you may have.

**Line 13a** adds the expected income tax and the self-employment together.

**Line 13b** allows you to deduct any tax credits. Ask your accountant to see if you're eligible for any credits.

**Line 13c** subtracts the credits from the taxes owed for your total estimated tax.

**Line 14a** calculates 90% of the tax owed. If you pay at least 90% of the taxes owed, you will not be charged a penalty.

**Line 14b** requires the tax liability on your previous year's taxes unless you had an adjusted gross income (AGI) of more than $150,000 or you filed a joint return last year and won't be filing a joint return this year. If your AGI was over $150,000, you will calculate 110% of the previous year's tax. If you are changing your filing status, read Publication 505 to compute the amount due.

To compute the amount on Line 14b, follow the IRS instructions using your prior year tax return:

1. **Form 1040A**—the amount on line 39 reduced by the amount on line 38, and any refundable credits on lines 42a, 43, 44, and 45.

2. **Form 1040EZ**—the amount on line 12 reduced by the amount on lines 8a and 11.
3. **Form 1040**—the amount on line 63 reduced by:
   a.  Unreported Social Security and Medicare tax or RRTA tax from Form 1040, line 58;
   b.  Any tax included on line 59 on excess contributions to an IRA, Archer MSA, Coverdell education savings account, health savings account, ABLE account, or on excess accumulations in qualified retirement plans;
   c.  Any shared responsibility payment on line 61;
   d.  Amounts on line 62 as listed under Exception 2, earlier; and
   e.  Any refundable credit amounts on lines 66a, 67, 68, 69, and 72, and credit from Form 8885 included on line 73.

For our example, we'll assume you paid $8000 last year.

**Line 14c** is the smaller of lines 14 a or b. This is the minimum amount the government expects you to pay in taxes without having to pay a penalty.

**Line 15** will be the amount of income tax you expect to have withheld from your regular paycheck plus any investment withholdings. If you haven't changed exemptions and don't expect your salary to change much, use the amount of withholding from the previous year. For this example, let's assume $4600.

**Line 16a** calculates the amount of estimated taxes you will need to pay over the year by taking the expected withholding away from the expected taxes, if the number is greater than zero, go to the next line.

---

### BANISH Bite #17

*Take the amount on Line 16a and divide it by 12. Every month, move those dollars to a savings account, so you are sure to have enough money to pay the quarterly taxes.*

---

**Line 16b** subtracts your expected withholding from the total estimated taxes on Line 13c. If it is less than $1000, you don't need to file any estimated tax payments. If it is more, go to the next line.

**Line 17** multiplies Line 16a (estimated taxes less estimated withholding) by .25 (25%) to calculate the quarterly payment. This will be the amount of the check you send to the IRS.

> ### BANISH Bite #18
> ### *Quarterly Tax Payments are due near the 15th of April, June, September, and January of the next year.*
> ### *Be sure to set up a calendar alert to remind you to send in your payment.*

The 1040 ES instructions at www.irs.gov/pub/irs-pdf/f1040es.pdf will give you the address to mail the payment based on the state you live in. It also has **Payment Vouchers** for you to complete and mail with your check, or you may pay online.

Tear off here

| Form 1040-ES Department of the Treasury Internal Revenue Service | 2017 Estimated Tax | Payment Voucher 4 OMB No. 1545-0074 |
|---|---|---|

File only if you are making a payment of estimated tax by check or money order. Mail this voucher with your check or money order payable to **"United States Treasury."** Write your social security number and "2017 Form 1040-ES" on your check or money order. Do not send cash. Enclose, but do not staple or attach, your payment with this voucher.

Calendar year—Due Jan. 16, 2018
Amount of estimated tax you are paying by check or money order.

| | Dollars | Cents |
|---|---|---|

| Print or type | Your first name and initial | Your last name | Your social security number |
|---|---|---|---|
| | If joint payment, complete for spouse | | |
| | Spouse's first name and initial | Spouse's last name | Spouse's social security number |
| | Address (number, street, and apt. no.) | | |
| | City, state, and ZIP code. (If a foreign address, enter city, also complete spaces below.) | | |
| | Foreign country name | Foreign province/county | Foreign postal code |

For Privacy Act and Paperwork Reduction Act Notice, see instructions.
-9-

Form 1040-ES (2017)

They also include a **Record of Estimated Tax Payments** for you to keep.

**Record of Estimated Tax Payments** (Farmers, fishermen, and fiscal year taxpayers, see *Payment Due Dates.*)

*Keep for Your Records*

| Payment number | Payment due date | (a) Amount due | (b) Date paid | (c) Check or money order number, or credit or debit card confirmation number | (d) Amount paid (do not include any convenience fee)* | (e) 2016 overpayment credit applied | (f) Total amount paid and credited (add (d) and (e)) |
|---|---|---|---|---|---|---|---|
| 1 | 4/18/2017 | | | | | | |
| 2 | 6/15/2017 | | | | | | |
| 3 | 9/15/2017 | | | | | | |
| 4 | 1/16/2018** | | | | | | |
| Total . . . . . . . . . . . . . . . . . . ▶ | | | | | | | |

\* You can deduct the convenience fee charged by the service provider in 2017 as a miscellaneous itemized deduction (subject to the 2%-of-AGI limit) on your 2017 income tax return.

\*\* You do not have to make this payment if you file your 2017 tax return by January 31, 2018, and pay the entire balance due with your return.

**BANISH Action Steps**

- *Set a designated time each week to focus on your bookkeeping.*
- *Design your chart of accounts.*
- *Learn what is deductible (see Appendix).*
- *Automate any recurring bills.*
- *Pay any other bills.*
- *Automate invoices to customers, if possible.*
- *Link your bank data to your accounting system to automatically record income and match to bills paid.*
- *Calculate your estimated taxes for the year using Form 1040 ES.*
- *Each month, put 1/12 of the estimated taxes into a savings account to pay the quarterly taxes.*

*Richard Pryor's defense for failing to file taxes was, "You know, I forgot."*

*The judge sentenced him to 10 days in jail, telling him he'd be sure to remember next time.*

# BANISH Step 5—Summarize Your Information

### A. The End of each Month

The end of the month is important because this is when you typically receive statements from your bank, credit card processors and providers, and vendors. I know the transactions are automatically being downloaded as they occur, and you have been religiously taking an hour every week or so to keep things organized, but month-end is the time to pull everything together and understand how your business is doing.

### 1) Preliminary steps

Start by **paying any outstanding bills**, giving special attention to any expenses that need to be charged to a customer or client.

Next, **download your banking** information or enter any automatic drafts from your bank statement into your system. Code them to the proper accounts for deductibility, and review for any that should be included on a client invoice. Any unknown charges should be investigated immediately.

**Import or enter all credit card charges**. Should any of them be charged to a client? Do you have receipts for all the deductible items? Are they coded to the correct account?

---

### BANISH Bite #19

*This is a good time to link those pictures of the receipts to the credit card charges and to code them correctly.*

---

**Calculate your mileage deduction** for the month. **The rates change every year, so check irs.gov** before making your calculation. You must document any miles you want to deduct, so either use an app on your phone or keep a mileage log in your car.

For business trips, you are allowed to deduct 53.5 cents (2017 rate) times the number of miles. If your office is outside your home, you cannot deduct the commuting miles, but the miles driven to visit a client or to pick up product are allowed. Trips to the post office or to conferences are also considered business miles. If you are an Uber or Lyft driver, be sure to track the miles driven to pick up passengers as well as the actual mileage during the ride.

Calculating your actual vehicle expenses may give you a larger deduction. You must track business and personal miles and allocate the expense based on the percentage used. Actual vehicle expenses include: depreciation or lease payments, registration fees, licenses, gas, insurance, repairs, oil, garage rent, tires, tolls, and parking fees. So, if your total vehicle expenses are $4000 per year, and you use the car for business 25% of the miles driven, you would have a $1000 deduction.

You cannot use both the standard mileage deduction and a percentage of the costs. For example, if you are using the standard mileage deduction, none of the car insurance is deductible.

## BANISH Bite #20

*You can also deduct the miles driven for medical appointments or moving purposes at a lower rate (17 cents per mile in 2017). Miles driven while volunteering for a charitable organization can be charged at 14 cents per mile.*

Now that all your expenses are recorded, you should review your income. **Invoice all customers or clients**, including the mileage and other expenses as appropriate. Next, **import or enter any e-commerce or sharing economy income** as we discussed in the previous chapter.

### 2) Bank reconciliation

It's time to **reconcile your bank account** to the cash account in your accounting system. Don't assume that just because you're using the automatic downloads, that the account will reconcile.

If you're using Quicken, QuickBooks, or something similar, there will be a reconciliation option usually under the Banking or Tools menu. Follow their instructions, but they will be like the steps you follow to reconcile manually.

The example on the next page shows the bank and the accounting system with only a $3.00 difference. But when you review the details, you see that there is a $37 outstanding check that will clear the bank statement next month.

---

### BANISH Bite #21

*Don't just look at the balance on the bank statement and think, "It's only a few dollars different than my accounting system, so I don't need to reconcile it."*

*There may be missing items that cancel each other out, causing you to lose a deduction and make reconciling in the future much more difficult.*

---

The bank is also showing a $40 withdrawal for a mobile phone bill. You need to record the phone expense in your system. If you had assumed the bank was reconciled "close enough," you would have missed the telephone expense (which is probably deductible), and next month, when check # 1003 clears the bank, it would be difficult to figure out why you can't reconcile.

**Bank Reconciliation**

| | | Date | Per Bank | Per My Books | Difference |
|---|---|---|---|---|---|
| Starting Balance | | 1-Jan | $ - | $ - | $ - |
| **Deposits** | | | | | |
| Uber | | 5-Jan | $ 99.00 | $ 99.00 | $ - |
| Uber | | 12-Jan | 57.00 | 57.00 | - |
| Uber | | 19-Jan | 125.00 | 125.00 | - |
| Uber | | 26-Jan | 95.00 | 95.00 | - |
| Total Deposits | | | $ 376.00 | $ 376.00 | $ - |
| **Checks paid** | | | | | |
| | 1001 | 2-Jan | (50.00) | (50.00) | - |
| | 1002 | 10-Jan | (28.00) | (28.00) | - |
| | 1003 | 31-Jan | [     ] | (37.00) | 37.00 |
| Total Checks | | | $ (78.00) | $ (115.00) | $ 37.00 |
| **Other Withdrawals** | | | | | |
| Mobile Phone | | | $ (40.00) | [     ] | $ (40.00) |
| Total Checks and withdrawals | | | $ (118.00) | $ (115.00) | $ (3.00) |
| | | | | | $ - |
| Cash Balance | | | $ 258.00 | $ 261.00 | $ (3.00) |

To reconcile your account, start with an opening balance. If you have just opened a checking account, this will be $0. If you're using a current account that has never been reconciled, start with the bank balance from the previous month.

The basics of reconciling your checking account is to take the Bank Balance at the end of the month, add any deposits you made that the bank has not yet recorded (Outstanding Deposits), and subtract any checks or withdrawals you made that have not yet cleared the bank (Outstanding Checks). The ending balance should equal what is in your accounting records. In this example, the balance in My Books is the $261 from above less the $40 mobile phone charge for the corrected balance of $221.00.

| | |
|---|---|
| Bank Balance | $ 258.00 |
| Plus Outstanding deposits | - |
| Less Outstanding Checks | (37.00) |
| Balance per My Books | 221.00 |

But sometimes it doesn't agree with the amount in your accounting system. If not, look at each step more closely. The bank statement will total Deposits, Credits, and Interest on your statement. Does that amount agree to the amount your checking account balance increased in your accounting system? If not, you may have an outstanding deposit or you may have forgotten to record a transfer in. Record in your accounting system any income you missed and see if the totals now match.

### BANISH Bite #22
*If your credit card processor takes out the merchant fees before transferring the money into your account, you'll need to adjust your accounting records to reflect this.*

Now do the same thing for the checks and withdrawals. Compare the bank's total for Checks and Withdrawals, less outstanding checks, to the total checks paid from the accounting system. If it doesn't match, you'll need to compare each transaction and record any missing ones.

Another reason the account may not reconcile is due to the Beginning Balance. Does the beginning balance equal last month's ending balance? You may have old outstanding checks or deposits coming through that may or may not have been recorded in your system.

Once you've investigated and made any corrections, save a copy of your bank reconciliation and the related bank statements to your Bank Statements file on your computer (which is also saved to the internet for backup). Do this every month, and errors will be easy to catch.

### 3) Credit card reconciliation

I'm sure you don't want to hear this, but you need to reconcile your credit card accounts each month, just like you do with your bank accounts. If you're entering the charges manually at the end of the month, you will be reconciling as you go. But if you enter or download the charges during the month, you need to be sure you've recorded them all and that the amount due is correct.

In most of the automated accounting systems, you'll reconcile the credit cards in the same manner as a bank account. Go to the Banking or Tools menu and look for a Reconciliation option. Then select the credit card account you want to reconcile. Because credit card statements are not usually dated the last day of the month, be sure to pay attention to the date. Treat any charges or payments after the statement date as outstanding items.

### 4) Sales tax payments

This can be a tricky area. Every state has different rules and requirements whether you sell only to local people or sell nationwide. Some states require sales tax to be paid on services as well as products, others don't. Before you start selling, learn the rules for your state and locality. Even if you don't collect the sales tax, if it is owed, you will have to pay it.

---

### BANISH Bite #23

*For your convenience, I have links to each state's Department of Revenue and Secretary of State websites at www.accountantbesideyou.com/state-weblinks.*

---

### 5) Financial statements

You have input all your data and reconciled all your accounts. Now let's run some reports to see how your business is doing. If you are using an automated system, there will be an area titled **Reports** which will give you ability to produce the financial statements I'll be explaining.

If you are using a manual system, you'll need to design your own on a spreadsheet program. The balance sheet and income statement examples below were prepared in a spreadsheet.

First, another quick accounting lesson on standard financial reports. If you have a loan from a bank, they may wish to see data in these formats.

The **Balance Sheet** is a snapshot of the company health as of a certain time. It shows what is owned (assets), what is owed (liabilities), and what is left over (owner's equity). The owner's equity includes net income for the year plus the accumulation of net incomes and losses for prior years.

If you are a freelancer with no inventory or equipment, your balance sheet may be as simple as this:

| BALANCE SHEET | |
| --- | --- |
| Assets: | |
| Cash | $ 950.00 |
| Total Assets | $ 950.00 |
| | |
| Liabilities and Owners Equity: | |
| Credit Card | $ 350.00 |
| Total Liability | $ 350.00 |
| | |
| Owner's Equity | $ 600.00 |
| Total Liability and Equity | $ 950.00 |

Note the Total Assets must equal the Total Liabilities and Equity.

If you have inventory, computers, and a line of credit, your balance sheet will be a bit longer.

| BALANCE SHEET | |
| --- | --- |
| Assets: | |
| Cash | $ 950.00 |
| Inventory | 2,300.00 |
| Equipment | 1,500.00 |
| Total Assets | $4,750.00 |
| | |
| Liabilities and Owners Equity: | |
| Credit Card | $ 350.00 |
| Bank Line of Credit | 2,000.00 |
| Total Liability | 2,350.00 |
| | |
| Owner's Equity | $2,400.00 |
| Total Liability and Equity | $4,750.00 |

The next most common statement is the **Income Statement** (or Profit & Loss). It shows your income and expenses over a period of time (i.e. weekly, monthly, quarterly, or annually). This report will show how much money you are making on your sales.

| INCOME STATEMENT | |
|---|---|
| For Month Ending January 31 | |
| Sales: | |
| Graphic design | 2,641.00 |
| | |
| Expenses: | |
| Advertising | 50.00 |
| Supplies | 100.00 |
| Mileage | 16.00 |
| Utilities-Website | 75.00 |
| Total expenses | 241.00 |
| Net Income | $2,400.00 |

This is where all the work you did setting up your chart of accounts pays off. You'll see immediately your expenses by deduction category. You can also design reports to show comparisons to prior months and years to spot any trends. In Step 6, I'll show you how to add budget data.

When using a computerized accounting package, look for the **Accounts Receivable Aging** report to see which customers have not yet paid their invoices and how long they have been outstanding.

### Larry's Landscaping & Garden Supply
### A/R Aging Summary
#### As of December 15, 2021

| | Current | 1 - 30 | 31 - 60 | 61 - 90 | > 90 | TOTAL |
|---|---|---|---|---|---|---|
| Adam's Candy Shop | 40.00 | 0.00 | 0.00 | 0.00 | 0.00 | 40.00 |
| Balak, Mike | 360.00 | 0.00 | 0.00 | 0.00 | 0.00 | 360.00 |
| Blackwell, Edward | 1,125.00 | 0.00 | 0.00 | 0.00 | 0.00 | 1,125.00 |
| Crenshaw, Bob | 1,591.03 | 0.00 | 0.00 | 0.00 | 0.00 | 1,591.03 |
| Ecker Design | 3,170.96 | 0.00 | 0.00 | 0.00 | 0.00 | 3,170.96 |
| Golliday Sporting Goods | 2,704.19 | 0.00 | 0.00 | 0.00 | 0.00 | 2,704.19 |
| Kummens, Susie | 1,515.56 | 0.00 | 0.00 | 0.00 | 0.00 | 1,515.56 |
| Stinson, Tracy | 1,730.30 | 0.00 | 0.00 | 0.00 | 0.00 | 1,730.30 |
| Theurer-Davis, Vicki | 907.29 | 0.00 | 0.00 | 0.00 | 0.00 | 907.29 |
| Walker, Rich | 185.00 | 0.00 | 0.00 | 0.00 | 0.00 | 185.00 |
| Williams, Abraham | 1,989.46 | 0.00 | 0.00 | 0.00 | 0.00 | 1,989.46 |
| TOTAL | 35,990.02 | 0.00 | 0.00 | 0.00 | 0.00 | 35,990.02 |

If you input your bills when you receive them, the **Accounts Payable Aging** report will tell you which bills are coming due and how much cash you will need for them.

### Larry's Landscaping & Garden Supply
### A/P Aging Summary
#### As of December 15, 2021

| | Current | 1 - 30 | 31 - 60 | 61 - 90 | > 90 | TOTAL |
|---|---|---|---|---|---|---|
| Cal Gas & Electric | ▶ 137.50 ◀ | 0.00 | 0.00 | 0.00 | 0.00 | 137.50 |
| Cal Telephone | 45.00 | 0.00 | 0.00 | 0.00 | 0.00 | 45.00 |
| Conner Garden Supplies | 127.20 | 0.00 | 0.00 | 0.00 | 0.00 | 127.20 |
| Nolan Hardware and Supp... | 610.00 | 336.00 | 0.00 | 0.00 | 0.00 | 946.00 |
| Robert Carr Masonry | 196.25 | 0.00 | 0.00 | 0.00 | 0.00 | 196.25 |
| Townley Insurance Agency | 427.62 | 0.00 | 0.00 | 0.00 | 0.00 | 427.62 |
| TOTAL | 1,543.57 | 336.00 | 0.00 | 0.00 | 0.00 | 1,879.57 |

Now you have a good idea of how much money you made (or lost) for the month and what money is expected to come in and go out.

### BANISH Bite #24
*Don't forget to set aside 1/12th of your estimated taxes each month.*

### B. The End of the Quarter

There are a few things that possibly need to be done quarterly. If you collect sales tax, many states allow you to file it quarterly instead of monthly. (Check out your state's Department of Revenue—links are at www.accountantbesideyou.com/state-weblinks.)

Remember the Form 1040 ES (Estimated Self-Employment Taxes) we filled out in the last step? Pay the quarterly tax near the 15th of April, June, September, and January. You can mail a check with the voucher as we discussed previously or file and pay online using **Direct Pay**.

The IRS Direct Pay option is simple. Go to www.irs.gov/payments/direct-pay. Select **Make a Payment**, and you'll see a screen similar to the one below.

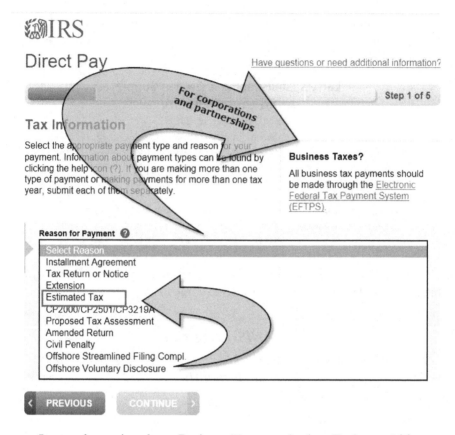

Ignore the notice about Business Taxes, and select **Estimated Tax** as your Reason for Payment. The screen will fill in the Form number and current year.

Once you select **Continue**, a pop-up box will ask if you want to continue. Select **Continue** and the system will ask you to **Verify Identity** by comparing a previously filed tax return. If you've never filed a return before, click on the **Have questions** link at the top of the page.

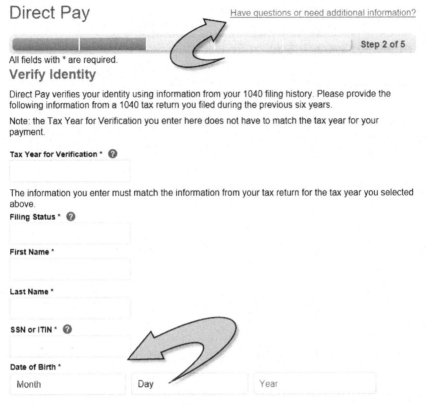

Fill in the requested information, including your Social Security number. If you do not have a Social Security number (i.e. a nonresident alien or a US resident alien), use your Individual Taxpayer Identification Number (ITIN) instead. After completing the form, select **Continue**.

The next page is for **Your Payment Information**.

# Direct Pay

Have questions or need additional information?

Step 3 of 5

All fields are required.

## Your Payment Information

Please enter and confirm the payment amount below.

The payment date below is the date you will get credit for the payment. If your payment is due today, schedule the next business day for your payment to avoid penalties and interest.

**Payment Amount** (example: 12345.00)

$

**Confirm Payment Amount**

$

**Payment Date** (within 30 days) ❓

02/17/2017

## Your Bank Account Information

**Routing Number**

**Account Type**
○ Checking
○ Savings

‹ PREVIOUS    CONTINUE ›

Cancel

*From the last line of Form 1040 ES.*

*Schedule the payment up to 30 days in advance.*

Enter the amount you calculated on Form 1040 ES, and select a payment date on or before the date due. You can fill out this form up to 30 days before the payment is submitted. Next, key in your banking information and **Continue.**

The same screen will appear with the following area to include your **Electronic Signature.**

Debit Authorization Agreement
☐ I accept the Debit Authorization Agreement.

## Electronic Signature

When you complete this electronic signature and select "Submit" below, your payment will be submitted.

**First Name**

**Last Name**

**SSN or ITIN** ❓

**Date**

‹ PREVIOUS    SUBMIT ›

After you read and accept the **Debit Authorization Agreement,** electronically sign the form and **Submit**. Your estimated taxes are paid.

Print or save a copy of the payment acknowledgement screen and save to your IRS folder.

### C. It's Year End. What Now?

Once you have finished all the regular monthly tasks for December, it's time to do a few additional tasks each year. Depending on the type of business you own, you may or may not have some of these expenses.

#### 1) Send 1099s to independent contractors

Before the end of January, you must send Form 1099 to any independent contractors you paid more than $600 throughout the year (check the IRS website for current levels). An independent contractor is an individual you pay for services that is not an employee. From the IRS website:

*People such as doctors, dentists, veterinarians, lawyers, accountants, contractors, subcontractors, public stenographers, or auctioneers who are in an independent trade, business, or profession in which they offer their services to the general public are generally independent contractors. However, whether these people are independent contractors or employees depends on the facts in each case. The general rule is that an individual is an independent contractor if the payer has the right to control or direct only the result of the work and not what will be done and how it will be done. The earnings of a person who is working as an independent contractor are subject to Self-Employment Tax.*

The key passage above is **if the payer has the right to control or direct only the result of the work and not what will be done and how it will be done.** In the simplest terms, this means you hire someone to do a specific job and pay them when it is finished.

The IRS assumes individuals working for a business are employees unless it is proven otherwise. When auditing an organization, they have a list of 20 questions to determine if the worker is an independent contractor or not.

In case you are wondering why it matters, income tax and payroll taxes are withheld on employees but not independent contractors. Independent contractors must pay the full (employee and employer) Social Security and Medicare taxes on their earnings. The IRS frowns upon businesses who classify workers as independent contractors to save on the additional employer payroll taxes.

> ### *Examples of a Contractor vs an Employee:*
>
> *A bookkeeper comes once a week to do the bookkeeping. If he has other clients, controls when the work will be done, and gives you the results (i.e. monthly financial statements), he is an independent contractor.*
>
> *If you require the bookkeeper to come in for a specified number of hours on a day you specify and give him detailed instructions on how to do the bookkeeping, he may be considered an employee.*
>
> *The gardener who uses his own equipment and is paid to keep the warehouse property mowed and clear of branches is treated as an independent contractor, as is the plumber.*
>
> *A receptionist who must answer the phones from your office during specific hours is an employee as he does not have the right to control or direct the work.*

### W-9 Request for Taxpayer Identification Number

If you have determined the person should be paid as an independent contractor, you will need to have him complete a W-9 Request for Taxpayer Identification Number. The form may be downloaded from the IRS website at www.irs.gov/pub/irs-pdf/fw9.pdf.

The contractor fills out the form with his own name or his business name, if applicable. He checks his type of business organization and his address. If he used his personal name, the SSN area should be completed. If he filled the form out as a business, he should use an EIN, if he has one.

The form must be signed and dated and returned to you. I require contractors to fill out the form before I will give them a check for their services.

### BANISH Bite #25

*You only need this form if you expect to pay the contractor at least $600 throughout the year. If you aren't sure, go ahead and have him complete it, so you won't have to track it down at year end.*

| Form **W-9** | **Request for Taxpayer** | Give Form to the |
|---|---|---|
| (Rev. December 2014) Department of the Treasury Internal Revenue Service | **Identification Number and Certification** | requester. Do not send to the IRS. |

**1** Name (as shown on your income tax return). Name is required on this line; do not leave this line blank.

**2** Business name/disregarded entity name, if different from above

**3** Check appropriate box for federal tax classification; check only **one** of the following seven boxes:

☐ Individual/sole proprietor or single-member LLC  ☐ C Corporation  ☐ S Corporation  ☐ Partnership  ☐ Trust/estate

☐ Limited liability company. Enter the tax classification (C=C corporation, S=S corporation, P=partnership) ▶ _____

**Note.** For a single-member LLC that is disregarded, do not check LLC; check the appropriate box in the line above for the tax classification of the single-member owner.

☐ Other (see instructions) ▶

**4** Exemptions (codes apply only to certain entities, not individuals; see instructions on page 3):

Exempt payee code (if any) _____

Exemption from FATCA reporting code (if any) _____

*(Applies to accounts maintained outside the U.S.)*

**5** Address (number, street, and apt. or suite no.)

Requester's name and address (optional)

**6** City, state, and ZIP code

**7** List account number(s) here (optional)

**Part I   Taxpayer Identification Number (TIN)**

Enter your TIN in the appropriate box. The TIN provided must match the name given on line 1 to avoid backup withholding. For individuals, this is generally your social security number (SSN). However, for a resident alien, sole proprietor, or disregarded entity, see the Part I instructions on page 3. For other entities, it is your employer identification number (EIN). If you do not have a number, see How to get a TIN on page 3.

**Note.** If the account is in more than one name, see the instructions for line 1 and the chart on page 4 for guidelines on whose number to enter.

**Social security number**

| | | | – | | | – | | | | |

or

**Employer identification number**

| | | – | | | | | | | |

*Fill out only one of these.*

**Part II   Certification**

Under penalties of perjury, I certify that:

1. The number shown on this form is my correct taxpayer identification number (or I am waiting for a number to be issued to me); and

2. I am not subject to backup withholding because: (a) I am exempt from backup withholding, or (b) I have not been notified by the Internal Revenue Service (IRS) that I am subject to backup withholding as a result of a failure to report all interest or dividends, or (c) the IRS has notified me that I am no longer subject to backup withholding; and

3. I am a U.S. citizen or other U.S. person (defined below); and

4. The FATCA code(s) entered on this form (if any) indicating that I am exempt from FATCA reporting is correct.

**Certification instructions.** You must cross out item 2 above if you have been notified by the IRS that you are currently subject to backup withholding because you have failed to report all interest and dividends on your tax return. For real estate transactions, item 2 does not apply. For mortgage interest paid, acquisition or abandonment of secured property, cancellation of debt, contributions to an individual retirement arrangement (IRA), and generally, payments other than interest and dividends, you are not required to sign the certification, but you must provide your correct TIN. See the instructions on page 3.

| **Sign Here** | **Signature of U.S. person ▶** | Date ▶ |

*Must be signed.*

## Form 1099-MISC

At year end, you'll need to fill out a **Form 1099-MISC** for each of the contractors whom you paid more than $600. If the service provider has incorporated, you do not need to send 1099s to any corporations. See example on the next page.

To fill out the form, your name (or your company name, if you have a DBA (doing business as)) goes at the top as the **PAYER**. Your SSN or EIN (employer identification number) goes in the **PAYER federal identification number**. The **Recipient's identification number** is the contractor's and should be copied from the W-9.

The majority of independent work will go into **Box 7 Nonemployee compensation**. Review the IRS instructions for Form 1099 to see if you need to report data in any of the other boxes.

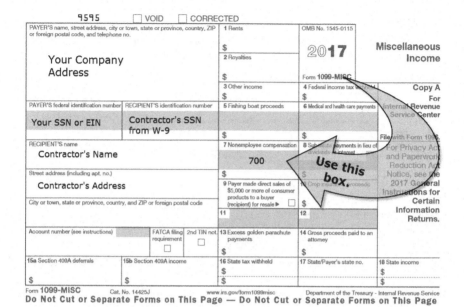

## BANISH Bite #26

*Send out the 1099s early in January, so if the contractors find any errors, they can be fixed before month end.*

Form 1099 has five copies—one for the IRS, one for your state tax department, two for the recipient, and one for you as the payer. You can print these out from www.irs.gov/pub/irs-pdf/f1099msc.pdf and send them to the contractors, but the IRS requires a red copy that cannot be printed from the website.

Once all the 1099s are completed and mailed out to the contractors, you will need to fill out **Form 1096 Annual Summary and Transmittal of U.S. Information Returns**.

### Form 1096 Annual Summary and Transmittal of U.S. Information Returns

This form sums up the total dollars sent on the 1099s. Your name and contact information goes at the top.

> ## BANISH Bite #27
>
> *Forms 1099 and 1096 are available at office supply stores in January, but save money by ordering them for free from the IRS.*
>
> www.irs.gov/businesses/online-ordering-for-information-returns-and-employer-returns
>
> *Order them in December to get them on time.*

Boxes 1 and 2—if you have an **Employer Identification Number,** use it; otherwise use your SSN. (This must be the number you used on the individual 1099s.) **Box 3** is the total number of forms. Please note that the 1099s have two forms per page. You want to count the number of FORMS not pages. **Box 4** reflects any federal income tax you withheld from the payments. I'm assuming you did not need to do this. **Box 5** is the total amount reported with this form. Calculate this amount by adding all the amounts on the individual 1099s together.

**Box 6** asks you to enter an X in the type of form being filed. You will choose 1099-MISC 95. Sign it with your title and date. Mail it with the red copies of the 1099 by the end of January.

---

### BANISH Bite #28

*Order extra copies of Form 1096 from the IRS when you order the 1099s in case of errors.*

---

Check with your state's Department of Revenue to see if, and when, you need to submit 1099s.

### 2) 1099s you receive

You may receive 1099s as well as send them, especially if you're a freelancer. Be sure to review these carefully and make certain they are accurate. If you find an error, call your client to determine if it is your mistake or theirs. They may need to reissue you a **CORRECTED 1099**.

Sometimes the difference is timing. You are probably using the cash basis of accounting. (Remember the accounting lesson at the beginning of the book? You recognize the income when you receive the cash, not when you do the work.) Your client may have cut the check on December 31, but you didn't get it until January. If that's the difference, there is no reason for a corrected 1099. You will need to document it, in case the IRS asks about it.

There are two main types of 1099s you may receive. The 1099 MISC, like the ones we discussed in the previous section, and **1099-K Payment Card and Third Party Network Transactions**. The 1099-K is the form you'll receive from your credit card processor and from companies like Uber.

**Box 1a Gross amount of payment** should tie to the amount of money you received from the processor. The form will also show the number of transactions and transaction totals by month.

Any discrepancies should be investigated immediately by calling the sender.

**3) Inventory count and adjustment**

If your business requires you to maintain an inventory of product, you will need to do a physical count at the end of the year to accurately measure your cost of goods sold. The count can be hand written on a piece of paper or input into a spreadsheet.

Perhaps you're a writer and you keep copies of each of your books on hand to sell at speaking engagements. The publisher sells you Book 1 for $4.50 a copy, and it costs an additional 50 cents per copy to ship it to you. The cost of the book is then $5.00. When you purchased the books, you charged the books and the shipping to the inventory account on the balance sheet (1xxx Book Inventory).

Each type of product needs to be counted separately and multiplied by its cost. Here is an example using three books with a total inventory of $809.

| Description | Number of Books | Cost | Inventory Value |
|---|---|---|---|
| Book 1 | 55 | $ 5.00 | $ 275.00 |
| Book 2 | 38 | $ 4.50 | $ 171.00 |
| Book 3 | 66 | $ 5.50 | $ 363.00 |
| | | | $ 809.00 |

Next you'll need to adjust your inventory for the ending balance. This is also required on **Schedule C-Part III Cost of Goods Sold**, which takes you through the steps required.

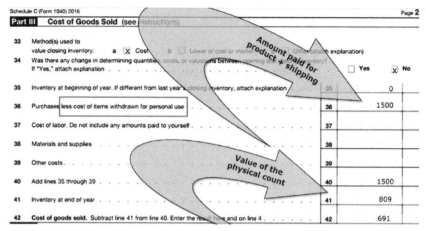

Schedule C (Form 1040) 2016      Page **2**

**Part III**   **Cost of Goods Sold (see** instructions)

| | | |
|---|---|---|
| 33 | Method(s) used to value closing inventory:   a [X] Cost   b [ ] Lower of cost or market   c [ ] Other (attach explanation) | |
| 34 | Was there any change in determining quantities, costs, or valuations between opening and closing inventory? If "Yes," attach explanation | [ ] Yes   [X] No |
| 35 | Inventory at beginning of year. If different from last year's closing inventory, attach explanation | 35   0 |
| 36 | Purchases less cost of items withdrawn for personal use | 36   1500 |
| 37 | Cost of labor. Do not include any amounts paid to yourself | 37 |
| 38 | Materials and supplies | 38 |
| 39 | Other costs | 39 |
| 40 | Add lines 35 through 39 | 40   1500 |
| 41 | Inventory at end of year | 41   809 |
| 42 | **Cost of goods sold.** Subtract line 41 from line 40. Enter the result here and on line 4 | 42   691 |

**Line 33** asks what method you use to value your inventory. The most common method is **a. Cost**. This is calculated as we discussed above by taking the cost from your supplier as the cost of the product. The next option, **b. Lower of cost or market**, is used by sellers whose products decline in value (i.e. if you had purchased a large batch of the latest iPhone to resell, but still had some left a year later).

**Line 34** asks about changes in inventory methods.

**Line 35** is the value of your beginning inventory. If this is not your first year to show an inventory, the beginning balance should be equal to the ending balance shown on the previous year's return.

**Line 36** is your purchases less the value of any of the items you used personally. For the book's example, we are using, you would need to reduce the cost of the purchases by any books you pulled out to give to your family.

**Lines 37-39** are used if you make products. If you make earrings to sell on Etsy and pay a friend to help assemble them, your purchases on Line 35 would include the beads, wire, etc. Lines 37-39 would include payments to your friend (but not to you—as an owner, that will be a Draw) and consumable supplies directly related to the production of the product.

**Line 40** adds the costs together for a total cost of your inventory.

**Line 41** is the value of the inventory counted at the end of the year. From our spreadsheet, pull the $809.

**Line 42** subtracts the ending inventory from the total cost of the inventory to calculate the **Cost of Goods Sold**. Later, we will input this number on Line 4 of the Schedule C.

Next you will need to adjust your inventory balance in your accounting system. This is usually done via a journal entry, unless you have a system that tracks individual inventory items.

A journal entry is simply a way to record increases and decreases in accounts. Remember that every transaction has two sides. In automated systems, the system automatically adjusts the cash account for deposits, checks, and other items that impact cash.

For non-cash items, the system needs to know where to post both sides of the entry. To adjust the inventory, we need to charge the cost of goods sold. The journal entry would look like this:

| Account | Debit | Credit |
|---|---|---|
| Cost of Goods Sold (5xxx) | $ 691.00 | |
| Inventory (1xxx) | | $ 691.00 |

If you are using a spreadsheet or manual program, for this example, you will add a line increasing the cost of goods sold account and reducing the inventory by the same amount. Your cash balance will not change.

### 4) Depreciation

Depreciation is the recognition that an asset (a computer, production equipment, or vehicle) declines in value over time. The IRS assumes that if you purchase a business asset with an expected useful life of two years or more, you should depreciate it over time instead of deducting the expense all at once. This does not apply to land, because land does not wear out or become obsolete.

At the end of the year, review your large purchases to see if they should be considered supplies (typically used within a year) or equipment (an asset with a life of at least two years). If there are any that should be depreciated, you'll need to fill out **Form 4562 Depreciation and Amortization** before calculating your business income.

Don't let the size of the form intimidate you. Unless you have more than $500,000 of depreciation expense, you'll only need to focus on the **Section 179** items. And if you have more than $500,000 of depreciation expense, you really should be having a CPA do your taxes for you.

**Part I—Election To Expense Certain Property Under Section 179** refers to the section of the IRS code that allows you to take the entire cost of the item in the year of purchase. Note it asks you to go to **Part V** first if you have **Listed Property**. Listed property refers primarily to vehicles. If you own a car and plan on charging depreciation instead of using the standard mileage deduction, it will be entered here. If you run a charter boat service, the purchase of the boat would be under listed property.

**Line 6** will list the items purchased with the same cost in both columns b and c. If you have more than two pieces of equipment, write SEE ATTACHED SCHEDULE and list the totals. Don't forget to attach the schedule with the items and their costs.

| Form **4562** | **Depreciation and Amortization** | OMB No. 1545-0172 |
|---|---|---|
| | (Including Information on Listed Property) | **2016** |
| Department of the Treasury Internal Revenue Service (99) | ► Attach to your tax return. ► Information about Form 4562 and its separate instructions is at *www.irs.gov/form4562.* | Attachment Sequence No. **179** |
| Name(s) shown on return | Business or activity to which this form relates | Identifying number |

**Part I**  Election To Expense Certain Property Under Section 179
Note: *If you have any listed property, complete Part V before you complete Part I.*

| 1 | Maximum amount (see instructions) | | 1 | |
|---|---|---|---|---|
| 2 | Total cost of section 179 property placed in service (see instructions) | | 2 | |
| 3 | Threshold cost of section 179 property before reduction in limitation (see instructions) | | 3 | |
| 4 | Reduction in limitation. Subtract line 3 from line 2. If zero or less, enter -0- | | 4 | |
| 5 | Dollar limitation for tax year. Subtract line 4 from line 1. If zero or less, enter -0-. If married filing separately, see instructions | | 5 | |

| 6 | (a) Description of property | (b) Cost (business use only) | (c) Elected cost |
|---|---|---|---|
| | | | |
| | | | |

| 7 | Listed property. Enter the amount from line 29 | | 7 | | |
|---|---|---|---|---|---|
| 8 | Total elected cost of section 179 property. Add amounts in column (c), lines 6 and 7 | | | 8 | |
| 9 | Tentative deduction. Enter the **smaller** of line 5 or line 8 | | | 9 | |
| 10 | Carryover of disallowed deduction from line 13 of your 2015 Form 4562 | | | 10 | |
| 11 | Business income limitation. Enter the smaller of business income (not less than zero) or line 5 (see instructions) | | | 11 | |
| 12 | Section 179 expense deduction. Add lines 9 and 10, but don't enter more than line 11 | | | 12 | |
| 13 | Carryover of disallowed deduction to 2017. Add lines 9 and 10, less line 12 ► | | 13 | | |

Note: *Don't use Part II or Part III below for listed property. Instead, use Part V.*

**Part II**  Special Depreciation Allowance and Other Depreciation (Don't include listed property.) (See instructions.)

14 ~~Special depreciation allowance for qualified property~~ ~~other than listed property~~ ~~placed in s~~

| c 40-year | | 40 yrs. | M/M | S/L | |
|---|---|---|---|---|---|

**Part IV**  Summary (See instructions.)

| 21 | Listed property. Enter amount from line 28 | | 21 | |
|---|---|---|---|---|
| 22 | **Total.** Add amounts from line 12, lines 14 through 17, lines 19 and 20 in column (g), and line 21. Enter here and on the appropriate lines of your return. Partnerships and S corporations—see instructions | | 22 | |
| 23 | For assets shown above and placed in service during the current year, enter the portion of the basis attributable to section 263A costs | 23 | | |

For Paperwork Reduction Act Notice, see separate instructions.    Cat. No. 12906N    Form **4562** (2016)

---

Form 4562 (2016)    Page **2**

**Part V**  Listed Property (Include automobiles, certain other vehicles, certain aircraft, certain computers, and property used for entertainment, recreation, or amusement.)

Note: *For any vehicle for which you are using the standard mileage rate or deducting lease expense, complete only 24a, 24b, columns (a) through (c) of Section A, all of Section B, and Section C if applicable.*

**Section A—Depreciation and Other Information (Caution: See the instructions for limits for passenger automobiles.)**

24a Do you have evidence to support the business/investment use claimed? ☐ Yes ☐ No   24b If "Yes," is the evidence written? ☐ Yes ☐ No

| (a) Type of property (list vehicles first) | (b) Date placed in service | (c) Business/ investment use percentage | (d) Cost or other basis | (e) Basis for depreciation (business/investment use only) | (f) Recovery period | (g) Method/ Convention | (h) Depreciation deduction | (i) Elected section 179 cost |
|---|---|---|---|---|---|---|---|---|
| 25 Special depreciation allowance for qualified listed property placed in service during the tax year and used more than 50% in a qualified business use (see instructions) . | | | | | | | 25 | |
| 26 Property used more than 50% in a qualified business use: | | | | | | | | |
| | | % | | | | | | |
| | | % | | | | | | |
| | | % | | | | | | |
| 27 Property used 50% or less in a qualified business use: | | | | | | | | |
| | | % | | | S/L – | | | |
| | | % | | | S/L – | | | |
| | | % | | | S/L – | | | |
| 28 Add amounts in column (h), lines 25 through 27. Enter here and on line 21, page 1 | | | | | 28 | | | |
| 29 Add amounts in column (i), line 26. Enter here and on line 7, page 1 | | | | | | | 29 | |

**Section B—Information on Use of Vehicles**

Complete this section for vehicles used by a sole proprietor, partner, or other "more than 5% owner," or related person. If you provided vehicles to your employees, first answer the questions in Section C to see if you meet an exception to completing this section for those vehicles.

| | | (a) Vehicle 1 | | (b) Vehicle 2 | | (c) Vehicle 3 | | (d) Vehicle 4 | | (e) Vehicle 5 | | (f) Vehicle 6 | |
|---|---|---|---|---|---|---|---|---|---|---|---|---|---|
| 30 | Total business/investment miles driven during the year (don't include commuting miles) | | | | | | | | | | | | |
| 31 | Total commuting miles driven during the year | | | | | | | | | | | | |
| 32 | Total other personal (noncommuting) miles driven | | | | | | | | | | | | |
| 33 | Total miles driven during the year. Add lines 30 through 32 | | | | | | | | | | | | |
| 34 | Was the vehicle available for personal use during off-duty hours? | Yes | No | Yes | No | Yes | No | Yes | No | Yes | No | Yes | No |
| 35 | Was the vehicle used primarily by a more than 5% owner or related person? | | | | | | | | | | | | |
| 36 | Is another vehicle available for personal use? | | | | | | | | | | | | |

~~Section C—Questions for Employers Who Provide Vehicles for Use by Their Employees~~

| 44 | Total. Add amounts in column (f). See the instructions for where to report | | 44 | |
|---|---|---|---|---|

Form **4562** (2016)

**Line 7** will be blank unless you are depreciating your car or other listed item. Read the IRS instructions for more details.

**Line 8** adds the equipment purchased to the listed property.

**Line 9** is the smaller of Line 5 or Line 8.

**Line 10** allows you to carryover any deduction not allowed in the previous year.

**Line 11** should be Gross Income from Line 7 on the Schedule C.

**Line 12** is the amount of the Section 179 expense deduction. Enter the smaller of Lines 9 and 10 added together or Line 11. You can't take a deduction for more depreciation than your gross income.

**Line 13** calculates the carryover of the disallowed if Lines 9 and 10 were greater than Line 11.

**Part IV—Summary**

If you had listed property, enter it on **Line 21.**

**Line 22** is the total deduction you will be allowed. Add Line 12 and Line 21. The total will be entered on **Schedule C, Line 13**.

**5) Completing the federal tax returns**

You've finished all your record keeping and made all your adjustments. It's time to fill out the necessary tax forms. If you had income from self-employment of at least $400, you will be required to file **Form 1040** (instead of the more simplified 1040EZ or 1040A).

> *If your business is considered a hobby (see Step 1), enter the net profit on Form 1040, Line 21. Do not use Schedule C or C-EZ.*

**Schedule C-EZ—Net Profit From Business**

**Schedule C or C-EZ** is the required schedule to show business income and expense. Use **Schedule C-EZ** if you don't have employees, inventory, depreciation, a loss, or expenses over $5000. If you can't use C-EZ, jump ahead to page 82.

At the very top of the form, you will put your name and SSN as **The Proprietor.**

## Part I—General information

**Line A** requires a description of your business, i.e. internet sales of crafts to the public.

**Line B** is looking for the six-digit **Principal Business or Professional Activity Code** (www.irs.gov/instructions/i1040sc/ch02.html#d0e2016). Select the one that is closest to your business description.

**Line C** is your business name, if you have one. If not, leave it blank.

**Line D** is ONLY for an Employer Identification Number. If you don't have one, leave it blank. Do not enter your SSN here.

**Line E** reflects your physical business address. If using your home address that will be on the 1040, leave this blank. The IRS does not want a post office box number.

**Line F** asks about the 1099s. Mark the **Yes** box if they were required.

**Line G** wants to know if you filed your 1099s. Of course, you will have.

## Part II—Figure Your Net Profit

**Part II** is where you'll report your income and expenses. Even though you aren't listing the expenses separately as you would on the Long Schedule, the rules for the deductibility of the expenses are the same.

**Line 1** is the gross receipts. This is **all** the business income you received, not your W-2 from an employer or other payments. Be sure to add up all your 1099s received to be certain they are included.

**Line 2** totals all your business expenses. Review the expense listing in the Appendix to be sure you understand what is deductible (especially if you have meals and entertainment). Even though the form is only asking for one number, you need all the documentation behind it.

If your total expenses are more than $5000, you must use Schedule C instead.

**Line 3** subtracts the expenses from the income for the **Net Profit**. You will enter this amount on **Form 1040 Line 12** and on **Schedule SE, Line 2**.

---

### BANISH Tip # 29

*Report all income even if you did not receive a 1099. If the client realizes their mistake and files a correction, the IRS may come back to look at your account.*

---

| SCHEDULE C-EZ<br>(Form 1040)<br><br>Department of the Treasury<br>Internal Revenue Service (99) | **Net Profit From Business**<br>(Sole Proprietorship)<br><br>▶ Partnerships, joint ventures, etc., generally must file Form 1065 or 1065-B.<br>▶ Attach to Form 1040, 1040NR, or 1041. ▶ See instructions on page 2. | OMB No. 1545-0074<br><br>**2016**<br>Attachment<br>Sequence No. 09A |
|---|---|---|
| Name of proprietor | | Social security number (SSN) |

**Part I  General Information**

| **You May Use Schedule C-EZ Instead of Schedule C Only If You:** | • Had business expenses of $5,000 or less,<br>• Use the cash method of accounting,<br>• Did not have an inventory at any time during the year,<br>• Did not have a net loss from your business,<br>• Had only one business as either a sole proprietor, qualified joint venture, or statutory employee. | **And You:** | • Had no employees during the year,<br>• Do not deduct expenses for business use of your home,<br>• Do not have prior year unallowed passive activity losses from this business, and<br>• Are not required to file Form 4562, Depreciation and Amortization, for this business. See the instructions for Schedule C, line 13, to find out if you must file. |
|---|---|---|---|

A  Principal business or profession, including product or service

B  Enter business code (see page 2) ▶

C  Business name. If no separate business name, leave blank.

D  Enter your EIN (see page 2)

E  Business address (including suite or room no.). Address not required if same as on page 1 of your tax return.

City, town or post office, state, and ZIP code

F  Did you make any payments in 2016 that would require you to file Form(s) 1099? (see the instructions for Schedule C)  ☐ Yes  ☐ No

G  If "Yes," did you or will you file required Forms 1099?  ☐ Yes  ☐ No

*Only business income*

**Part II  Figure Your Net Profit**

1  **Gross receipts. Caution:** If this income was reported to you on Form W-2 and the "Statutory employee" box on that form was checked, see *Statutory employees* in the instructions for Schedule C, line 1, and check here  ▶ ☐  | **1** |

2  **Total expenses** (see page 2). If more than $5,000, you **must** use Schedule C  | **2** |

3  **Net profit.** Subtract line 2 from line 1. If less than zero, you **must** use Schedule C. Enter on both **Form 1040, line 12,** and **Schedule SE, line 2,** or on **Form 1040NR, line 13,** and **Schedule SE, line 2** (see page 2). (Statutory employees **do not** report this amount on Schedule SE, line 2.) Estates and trusts, enter on **Form 1041, line 3**  | **3** |

**Part III  Information on Your Vehicle.** Complete this part **only** if you are claiming car or truck expenses on line 2.

4  When did you place your vehicle in service for business purposes? (month, day, year) ▶ ....................... .

5  Of the total number of miles you drove your vehicle during 2016, enter the number of miles you used your vehicle for:

a  Business ....................  b  Commuting (see page 2) ....................  c  Other ....................

6  Was your vehicle available for personal use during off-duty hours?  ☐ Yes  ☐ No

7  Do you (or your spouse) have another vehicle available for personal use?  ☐ Yes  ☐ No

8a  Do you have evidence to support your deduction?  ☐ Yes  ☐ No

b  If "Yes," is the evidence written?  ☐ Yes  ☐ No

## Part III—Information on Your Vehicle

**Part III** is only necessary if you are including mileage or car expenses in your **Line 2 Total expenses** amount. Answer the questions on **Lines 4-8b** as completely as possible and be sure to keep your documentation.

Next, I'll walk you through the longer Schedule C.

## Schedule C—Profit or Loss From Business

**Schedule C** is required for most businesses. I'll take you step by step through it now. We'll start with page 1, which is shown on the following page.

At the very top of the form, you'll put your name and SSN as **The Proprietor.**

**Line A** requires a description of your business, i.e. internet sales of crafts to the general public.

**Line B** is looking for the six-digit **Principal Business or Professional Activity Code** (www.irs.gov/instructions/i1040sc/ch02.html#d0e2016). Select the one that is closest to your business description.

**Line C** is your business name, if you have one. If not, leave it blank.

**Line D** is ONLY for an Employer Identification Number. If you don't have one, leave it blank. Do not enter your SSN here.

**Line E** reflects your physical business address. If using your home address that will be on the 1040, leave this blank. The IRS does not want a post office box number.

**Line F** is your accounting method. Most of you will select **(1) Cash.**

**Line G** wants to know if you are the one running the business. Select **Yes** or follow the instructions related to limitations on losses.

**Line H** wants to know if this is a new business.

**Line I** asks about the 1099s. Mark the **Yes** box if they were required.

**Line J** wants to know if you filed your 1099s. Of course, you will have.

### Part I—Income

**Part I** shows your receipts and cost of goods sold. On **Line 1**, report the income received. Be sure to add all 1099s (including 1099-K and 1099-Misc). If you found a timing difference, explain the variance on an attached note.

**Line 2** reflects cash or credits issued to customers for returns.

**Line 3** subtracts the returns from the income for a net sales number.

**Line 4** is the cost of goods sold amount from the worksheet on **Part III** of Schedule C as we discussed on page 76. If you do not have inventory, this will be left blank.

**Line 5** calculates **Gross profit** by subtracting cost of goods sold from the net sales.

**Line 6** is for income received not directly related to your services or products. It includes interest income from your business checking or investment accounts, prizes or awards you may have received, fuel tax refunds, and other various items. Check with your accountant if you have large amounts that seem to go here.

**Line 7** calculates **Gross income** by adding gross profit and other income together.

| SCHEDULE C (Form 1040) | **Profit or Loss From Business** (Sole Proprietorship) | OMB No. 1545-0074 |
|---|---|---|
| Department of the Treasury Internal Revenue Service (99) | ▶ Information about Schedule C and its separate instructions is at *www.irs.gov/schedulec*. ▶ Attach to Form 1040, 1040NR, or 1041; partnerships generally must file Form 1065. | 20**16** Attachment Sequence No. **09** |

Name of proprietor | Social security number (SSN)

**A** Principal business or profession, including product or service (see instructions) | **B** Enter code from instructions ▶

**C** Business name. If no separate business name, leave blank. | **D** Employer ID number (EIN), (see instr.)

**E** Business address (including suite or room no.) ▶
City, town or post office, state, and ZIP code

**F** Accounting method: (1) ☐ Cash (2) ☐ Accrual (3) ☐ Other (specify) ▶

**G** Did you "materially participate" in the operation of this business during 2016? If "No," see instructions for limit on losses . ☐ Yes ☐ No

**H** If you started or acquired this business during 2016, check here . . . . . . . ▶ ☐

**I** Did you make any payments in 2016 that would require you to file Form(s) 1099? (see instructions) . . . . ☐ Yes ☐ No

**J** If "Yes," did you or will you file required Forms 1099? . . . . . . . . . . . . . ☐ Yes ☐ No

**Include 1099s received.**

### Part I  Income

| | | | |
|---|---|---|---|
| 1 | Gross receipts or sales. See instructions for line 1 and check the box if this income was reported to you on Form W-2 and the "Statutory employee" box on that form was checked . . . . . ▶ ☐ | 1 | |
| 2 | Returns and allowances . . . . . . . . . . . . . . . . . | 2 | |
| 3 | Subtract line 2 from line 1 . . . . . . . . . . . . . . . . | 3 | |
| 4 | Cost of goods sold (from line 42) . . . . . . . . . . . . . . | 4 | |
| 5 | **Gross profit.** Subtract line 4 from line 3 . . . . . . . . . . . . | 5 | |
| 6 | Other income, including federal and state gasoline or fuel tax credit or refund (see instructions) . . | 6 | |
| 7 | **Gross income.** Add lines 5 and 6 . . . . . . . . . . . . ▶ | 7 | |

### Part II  Expenses. Enter expenses for business use of your home only on line 30.

| | | | | | | | |
|---|---|---|---|---|---|---|---|
| 8 | Advertising . . . . . | 8 | | 18 | Office expense (see instructions) | 18 | |
| 9 | Car and truck expenses (see instructions) . . . . . | 9 | | 19 | Pension and profit-sharing plans | 19 | |
| | | | | 20 | Rent or lease (see instructions): | | |
| 10 | Commissions and fees . | 10 | | a | Vehicles, machinery, and equipment | 20a | |
| 11 | Contract labor (see instructions) | 11 | | b | Other business property . . . | 20b | |
| 12 | Depletion . . . . | 12 | | 21 | Repairs and maintenance . . | 21 | |
| 13 | Depreciation and section 179 expense deduction (not included in Part III) (see instructions) . . . . . | 13 | | 22 | Supplies (not included in Part III) | 22 | |
| | | | | 23 | Taxes and licenses . . . . | 23 | |
| | | | | 24 | Travel, meals, and entertainment: | | |
| 14 | Employee benefit programs (other than on line 19) . . | 14 | | a | Travel . . . . . . . | 24a | |
| 15 | Insurance (other than health) | 15 | | b | Deductible meals and entertainment (see instructions) . | 24b | |
| 16 | Interest: | | | 25 | Utilities . . . . . . . | 25 | |
| a | Mortgage (paid to banks, etc.) | 16a | | 26 | Wages (less employment credits) | 26 | |
| b | Other . . . . . | 16b | | 27a | Other expenses (from line 48) | 27a | |
| 17 | Legal and professional services | 17 | | b | Reserved for future use | 27b | |

**Details on expenses are in the Appendix.**

| | | | |
|---|---|---|---|
| 28 | **Total expenses** before expenses for business use of home. Add lines 8 through 27a . . . . . ▶ | 28 | |
| 29 | Tentative profit or (loss). Subtract line 28 from line 7 . . . . . . . . . . | 29 | |
| 30 | Expenses for business use of your home. Do not report these expenses elsewhere. Attach Form 8829 unless using the simplified method (see instructions). **Simplified method filers only:** enter the total square footage of: (a) your home: _____ and (b) the part of your home used for business: _____. Use the Simplified Method Worksheet in the instructions to figure the amount to enter on line 30 . . . . | 30 | |
| 31 | **Net profit or (loss).** Subtract line 30 from line 29. | 31 | |
| | • If a profit, enter on both **Form 1040, line 12** (or **Form 1040NR, line 13**) and on **Schedule SE, line 2.** (If you checked the box on line 1, see instructions). Estates and trusts, enter on **Form 1041, line 3.** • If a loss, you **must** go to line 32. | | |
| 32 | If you have a loss, check the box that describes your investment in this activity (see instructions). | | |
| | • If you checked 32a, enter the loss on both **Form 1040, line 12,** (or **Form 1040NR, line 13**) and on **Schedule SE, line 2.** (If you checked the box on line 1, see the line 31 instructions). Estates and trusts, enter on **Form 1041, line 3.** • If you checked 32b, you **must** attach **Form 6198.** Your loss may be limited. | 32a ☐ All investment is at risk. 32b ☐ Some investment is not at risk. | |

**Easiest approach.**

**To 1040, Line 12.**

For Paperwork Reduction Act Notice, see the separate instructions. | Cat. No. 11334P | Schedule C (Form 1040) 2016

## Part II—Expenses

**Part II** reflects the expenses occurred in running your business. Because you may need to reference what can be deducted by category throughout the year, I have detailed what goes in each of the line items from Line 8 to Line 27a in section B of the Appendix.

**Line 28** totals all the expenses from lines 8-27.

**Line 29** subtracts total expenses (line 28) from gross income (line 7) to compute the **Tentative profit or (loss).**

**Line 30** is for the home office deduction. You may utilize this deduction if it's your principal place of business AND you use the space regularly and exclusively for conducting business. A part of a room is allowed if that space is only used for business.

There are two ways to claim the home office deduction. The first and easiest is the **Simplified Method**. Basically, you take the square footage of the dedicated space multiplied by $5 with a maximum of 300 square feet. There is a worksheet you'll need to fill out to calculate the deduction properly. It is included in the Appendix.

The second method is to fill out **Form 8829 Expenses for Business Use of Your Home** (www.irs.gov/pub/irs-pdf/f8829.pdf). A copy of this form is also found in the Appendix. On it, you will calculate depreciation and detail the other expenses related to your home. This will then be allocated to personal versus business use of the home.

> ### BANISH Bite #30
> *I recommend using the simplified version, unless your home expenses are significant enough to justify the time to fill out Form 8829*

If using the Simplified Method worksheet, enter the total square footage of your home and the part of your home used for business. Then enter the amount from Line 5 of the worksheet onto Line 30.

If you used Form 8829, enter the Line 35 onto Schedule C, Line 30.

**Line 31 Net profit or (loss)** subtracts the home office deduction from Line 29. If it is a positive number (a profit), enter the amount on **Form 1040, Line 12**. If it's a negative number (a loss), you'll need to go to the next line.

**Line 32** wants to know if your investment is at risk. Most likely the answer will be **32a All investment is at risk**, but if you have invested in the business with protections against loss by a guarantee, stop-loss agreement, or something similar, you would select **32b Some investment is not at risk**, and you'll be required to file **Form 6198 At-Risk Limitations**. Please see your tax advisor if you are unsure of your status.

Either way, the loss amount should be entered onto **Form 1040, Line 12**.

You have now completed your **Schedule C Profit or Loss from Business,** so it's time to fill out your annual self-employment tax form.

## Schedule SE Self-Employment Tax

**Schedule SE** has two options—a **Short Schedule** and a **Long Schedule**. If your self-employment earnings for all your businesses combined plus any wages equal less than $118,500, you can probably use the Short Schedule. Answer the questions at the top of the form to see which one you should use.

We'll start down the left-hand side of the questions by assuming you do not have wages from another job. It then asks if you are a **minister**. If so, I recommend reading my book, *Church Accounting—The How-To Guide for Small and Growing Churches*, which details how ministers should file their self-employment forms.

The next question is about **optional methods**. They are explained at www.irs.gov/pub/irs-pdf/i1040sse.pdf and relate to tax credits and farm income.

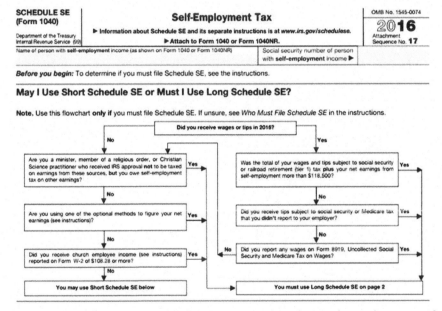

The last question on the left asks about **church employee income**. If you answered **No** to all these questions you, you may file the short form.

Now, let's look down the right-hand side. If you had wages from another job, were your wages and tips, plus net income of all your businesses (if you have more than one) more than $118,500? If so, you'll need to file the Long Schedule. If not, continue.

If you had unreported tips, you will need to file the Long Schedule. If not, the next question asks if you received money as an independent contractor but you believe the firm should have treated you as an employee. If so, you would have needed to file Form 8919 and will file the Long Schedule. More likely, the answer would be **No**, and you would continue down the list on the left to see if you could file the short form.

## Schedule SE Short Form

**Lines 1a** and **b** reflect farm and Social Security benefits.

**Line 2** is your business net profit or loss and comes from your Schedule C-EZ, Line 3 or C, Line 31.

**Line 3** adds the previous lines together.

**Line 4** will multiply Line 3 by .9235. If it's less than $400 and you don't have an amount on Line 1b, you don't need to file this form.

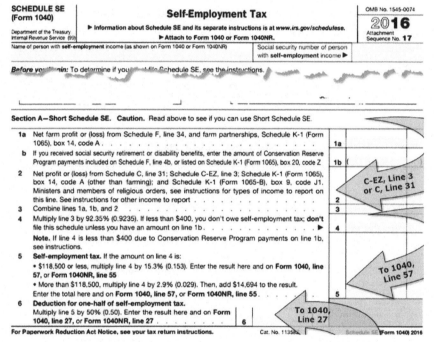

**Line 5** is the calculation of the self-employment tax. Multiply Line 4 by .153 (remember this is the employer and the employee portions of the tax). If Line 4 is greater than $118,500, you will multiply it by .029 and add $14,694. (This is because Social Security is not taxed above $118,500, but Medicare is.) Enter the calculated amount on **Form 1040, Line 57**.

**Line 6** calculates your deduction for the employer share of the self-employment tax. Multiply the amount on Line 5 by .50. This amount will also be reflected on **Form 1040, Line 27**.

In case you were not eligible to use the Short Schedule, we will now review the Long Schedule.

## Schedule SE Long Schedule

### Lines 1a and b reflect farm and Social Security benefits.

| Schedule SE (Form 1040) 2016 | Attachment Sequence No. **17** | | | Page **2** |
|---|---|---|---|---|
| Name of person with **self-employment** income (as shown on Form 1040 or Form 1040NR) | Social security number of person with **self-employment** income ▶ | | | |

**Section B—Long Schedule SE**

**Part I** **Self-Employment Tax**

**Note.** If your only income subject to self-employment tax is **church employee income**, see instructions. Also see instructions for the definition of church employee income.

**A** If you are a minister, member of a religious order, or Christian Science practitioner **and** you filed Form 4361, but you had $400 or more of **other** net earnings from self-employment, check here and continue with Part I . . . ▶ ☐

**1a** Net farm profit or (loss) from Schedule F, line 34, and farm partnerships, Schedule K-1 (Form 1065), box 14, code A. **Note.** Skip lines 1a and 1b if you use the farm optional method (see instructions) | **1a** |

**b** If you received social security retirement or disability benefits, enter the amount of Conservation Reserve Program payments included on Schedule F, line 4b, or listed on Schedule K-1 (Form 1065), box 20, code Z | **1b** | (    )

**2** Net profit or (loss) from Schedule C, line 31; Schedule C-EZ, line 3; Schedule K-1 (Form 1065), box 14, code A (other than farming); and Schedule K-1 (Form 1065-B), box 9, code J1. Ministers and members of religious orders, see instructions for types of income to report on this line. See instructions for other income to report. **Note.** Skip this line if you use the nonfarm optional method (see instructions) . . . . . . . . . . . . . . . . | **2** |

*C-EZ, Line 3 or C, Line 31*

**3** Combine lines 1a, 1b, and 2 . . . . . . . . . . . . . . . . . | **3** |

**4a** If line 3 is more than zero, multiply line 3 by 92.35% (0.9235). Otherwise, enter amount from line 3 | **4a** |

**Note.** If line 4a is less than $400 due to Conservation Reserve Program payments on line 1b, see instructions.

**b** If you elect one or both of the optional methods, enter the total of lines 15 and 17 here . . | **4b** |

**c** Combine lines 4a and 4b. If less than $400, **stop**; you do not owe self-employment tax. **Exception.** If less than $400 and you had **church employee income**, enter -0- and continue ▶ | **4c** |

**5a** Enter your **church employee income** from Form W-2. See instructions for definition of church employee income . . . | **5a** |

**b** Multiply line 5a by 92.35% (0.9235). If less than $100, enter -0- . . . . . . . . . . | **5b** |

**6** Add lines 4c and 5b . . . . . . . . . . . . . . . . . . . | **6** |

**7** Maximum amount of combined wages and self-employment earnings subject to social security tax or the 6.2% portion of the 7.65% railroad retirement (tier 1) tax for 2016 . . . . . . | **7** | 118,500 | 00 |

**8a** Total social security wages and tips (total of boxes 3 and 7 on Form(s) W-2) and railroad retirement (tier 1) compensation. If $118,500 or more, skip lines 8b through 10, and go to line 11 | **8a** |

**b** Unreported tips subject to social security tax (from Form 4137, line 10) | **8b** |

**c** Wages subject to social security tax (from Form 8919, line 10) | **8c** |

**d** Add lines 8a, 8b, and 8c . . . . . . . . . . . . . . . . . . | **8d** |

**9** Subtract line 8d from line 7. If zero or less, enter -0- here and on line 10 and go to line 11 . ▶ | **9** |

**10** Multiply the **smaller** of line 6 or line 9 by 12.4% (0.124) . . . . . . . . . . | **10** |

**11** Multiply line 6 by 2.9% (0.029) . . . . . . . . . . . . . . . . | **11** |

*To 1040, Line 57*

**12** **Self-employment tax.** Add lines 10 and 11. Enter here and on **Form 1040, line 57**, or **Form 1040NR, line 55** | **12** |

**13** Deduction for one-half of self-employment tax. Multiply line 12 by 50% (0.50). Enter the result here and on **Form 1040, line 27**, or **Form 1040NR, line 27** . . . . . . | **13** |

*To 1040, Line 27*

**Part II** **Optional Methods To Figure Net Earnings** (see instructions)

**Farm Optional Method.** You may use this method only if **(a)** your gross farm income¹ was not more than $7,560, **or (b)** your net farm profits² were less than $5,457.

**14** Maximum income for optional methods . . . . . . . . . . . . . . | **14** | 5,040 | 00 |

**15** Enter the **smaller** of: two-thirds (⅔) of gross farm income¹ (not less than zero) **or** $5,040. Also include this amount on line 4b above . . . . . . . . . . . . . . | **15** |

**Nonfarm Optional Method.** You may use this method only if **(a)** your net nonfarm profits³ were less than $5,457 and also less than 72.189% of your gross nonfarm income,⁴ and **(b)** you had net earnings from self-employment of at least $400 in 2 of the prior 3 years. **Caution.** You may use this method no more than five times.

**16** Subtract line 15 from line 14 . . . . . . . . . . . . . . . . | **16** |

**17** Enter the **smaller** of: two-thirds (⅔) of gross nonfarm income⁴ (not less than zero) **or** the amount on line 16. Also include this amount on line 4b above . . . . . . . . | **17** |

¹ From Sch. F, line 9, and Sch. K-1 (Form 1065), box 14, code B.
² From Sch. F, line 34, and Sch. K-1 (Form 1065), box 14, code A—minus the amount you would have entered on line 1b had you not used the optional method.
³ From Sch. C, line 31; Sch. C-EZ, line 3; Sch. K-1 (Form 1065), box 14, code A; and Sch. K-1 (Form 1065-B), box 9, code J1.
⁴ From Sch. C, line 7; Sch. C-EZ, line 1; Sch. K-1 (Form 1065), box 14, code C; and Sch. K-1 (Form 1065-B), box 9, code J2.

Schedule SE (Form 1040) 2016

**Line 2** is your business net profit or loss and comes from your Schedule C-EZ, Line 3 or C, Line 31.

**Line 3** adds the previous lines together.

**Line 4a** will multiply Line 3 by .9235. If it's less than $400 and you don't have an amount on Line 1b, you don't need to file this form.

**Line 4b and c** relates to the optional methods shown on Lines 14-17. Speak with your accountant, if you think these may be useful for you

**Line 5a and b** should be calculated if you have church employee income.

**Line 6** adds Lines 4c and 5b to see your total self-employment income.

**Line 7** is already filled in with the maximum earnings subject to Social Security tax.

**Lines 8a-d** is where you will report your wages and taxes received.

**Line 9** subtracts your wages from Line 7, the Social Security maximum.

**Line 10** has you multiply the smaller of Line 6 (self-employed earnings) or Line 9 by .124. This is the employer and employee portions of the Social Security tax.

**Line 11** multiplies Line 6 by .029—the employer and the employee portions of the Medicare tax.

**Line 12** is the calculation of the self-employment tax. Add lines 10 and 11. Enter the calculated amount on **Form 1040, Line 57**.

**Line 13** calculates your deduction for the employer share of the self-employment tax. Multiply the amount on Line 5 by .50. This amount will also be reflected on **Form 1040, Line 27**. That finishes up the Self-Employment Tax form.

**Form 1040 U.S. Individual Income Tax Return.**

> ### BANISH Bite #31
> *Before starting on your Form 1040, pull together all the tax documents you received in the mail or via email. Print out copies of your Schedule C or C-EZ and any other schedules you have prepared for easy reference.*

**Form 1040 U.S. Individual Income Tax Return** is referred to as "the long form" and has two pages. In the past, you may have filed the **1040EZ** or **1040A** (the short form), but if you have business income of more than $400, you must use the long form.

The 1040 encompasses everything that can go on an individual tax form, so I won't go over all lines. Instead, I'll show you which lines relate to your business.

The top section of Form 1040 is your taxpayer identification, filing status, and exemptions. The **Income** section includes your wages (Form W-2 from your employer), interest earned on savings and investments (Form 1099-INT), dividends (Form 1099-DIV), and alimony on **Lines 7-11.**

**Line 12** is your business income or loss from Schedule C-EZ, Line 3 or Schedule C, Line 31.

Lines **13** and **14** report your gains or losses on investments and property sold. Check with your tax advisor if you need assistance.

Lines **15-20** is for other areas of income, like IRAs, retirement, partnerships, farming, unemployment, and Social Security benefits.

**Line 21** is to capture any income not otherwise listed. This is where you record your net income if your business is considered a hobby instead of a business. Reread **BANISH Step 1** *Hobby or Business?* if you are still unsure.

**Line 22** adds Lines 7-21 for your **total income.**

The next section is titled **Adjusted Gross Income.** This is where the government allows you to take reductions from your income before calculating the tax.

Lines **23-26** are deductions for different occupations, health savings, and moving expenses.

**Line 27** is where you will deduct the portion of the self-employment tax you computed on Line 6 of the SE Short Schedule or Line 13 of the Long Schedule.

> ## Please Note:
> *Due to frequent changes in the tax law regarding health insurance and deductions, I am not covering it in this book. Please check with your accountant or www.irs.gov for the most updated requirements.*

**Line 28** refers to retirement plans available to the self-employed. If you have self-employment income, this can be a great way to save for retirement on a tax advantage basis.

Abby Eisenkraft is an Enrolled Agent—the highest credential the IRS awards—and the CEO of Choice Tax Solutions, Inc. Her great advice and wonderful sense of humor shines through in her book, *101 Ways to Stay off the IRS Radar*. I asked her to share her thoughts on SEPs (Simplified Employment Plans).

The IRS code isn't always cold and cruel – there's the SEP IRA deduction!

Many self-employed taxpayers don't have the benefit of a 401(k) plan. They can, of course, open a solo 401(k) plan, but the expense and administration discourage many taxpayers. The SEP IRA is a valuable alternative. Easy to set up, extra time to fund, no obligation to fund every year – all benefits.

If your business has profit, a SEP contribution can be made. If you have employees, the maximum is generally 25% of the W-2. For the owner, it's 20% of the net business income reduced by ½ of the self-employment tax.

You can make your SEP IRA contribution as late as April 15th of the following year. Also, if you file a valid extension, you have until October 15th to fund the SEP. This extra time is a great benefit for the self-employed taxpayer to be able to come up with the funds for the contribution. Contact your investment company for assistance with setting up your SEP-IRA.

You reduce your taxable income, you save money so you can eat later in life, and it is money that grows tax-deferred until it is tapped at retirement.

Check with your tax or investment advisor to see if a self-employment retirement plan could benefit you.

**Line 29** allows you to deduct the health insurance set up through your business.

**Lines 30-35** encompass a variety of other possible adjustments to gross income.

**Line 36** totals all the adjustments to income.

**Line 37** subtracts Line 36 from Line 22 for your **Adjusted Gross Income (AGI)**.

Now let's go to Page 2 of Form 1040. The top section of the second page of Form 1040 is **Tax and Credits**.

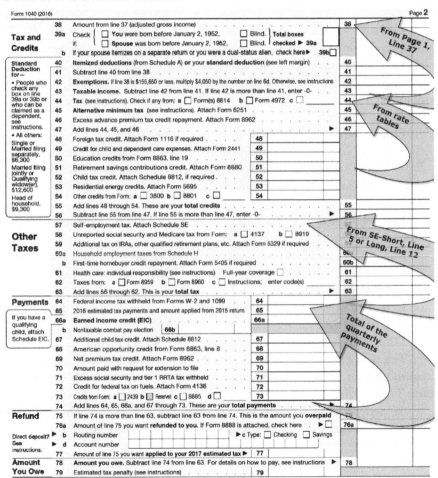

On **Line 38**, carry over the amount of AGI from Line 37 and answer the questions on **Line 39**.

**Line 40** allows you to enter the standard deduction (shown on the left margin) or itemize your deductions by including Schedule A. If you decide to itemize, remember your business expenses have already been included on Line 12 with your Schedule C, so be careful not to add them again.

**Line 41** subtracts your deductions from your AGI.

**Line 42** allows you $4050 multiplied by the number of exemptions from the first page unless your income is over $155,650.

**Line 43** subtract the exemption amount from Line 41 to get **Taxable income**.

**Line 44** is where you will enter the tax you calculate. Use the tax rate schedules like you did in Step 4 when you estimated your tax liability for the year.

**Lines 45-55** include the alternative minimum tax and various tax credits. You'll need to check with you accountant to see if any of them apply to you.

**Line 56** subtracts the total credits from the tax calculated on Line 47.

The next section is titled **Other Taxes**. The first line, **Line 57**, is the self-employment tax you calculated on Line 5 of the SE Short Schedule or Line 12 of the Long Schedule.

**Lines 58-62** include possible taxes from other sources.

**Lines 63** adds lines 56 through 62 to compute your **Total Tax.**

The next section is the **Payments**. Between your employer and your quarterly self-employment payments, you have probably already paid most of your taxes.

**Line 64** is the total of the federal income tax withheld from any W-2s or 1099s.

**Line 65** is the total of your quarterly payments plus any prior year refund you requested to be applied to this year's taxes. This allows you to make smaller quarterly payments.

**Line 66-73** relate to other credits and any payment you may have made if you filed an extension.

**Line 74** adds all the payments together for **Total Payments.**

The next part is the **Refund** section. If the total payments on Line 74 were more than the total tax on Line 63, you overpaid. Enter this amount on **Line 75.**

If there is a refund, you have several options. You can have them deposit the refund to more than one checking account by selecting **Line 76a** and filling out Form 8888.

By entering you bank routing and account number in **Lines 76b-d,** the IRS will deposit your refund directly into your account, or you can designate all or a portion of the refund to be applied to your next year's estimated taxes on **Line 77.**

> ### BANISH Bite #32
>
> *I know people think getting a big tax refund is great, but it really means the government had use of your cash instead of you.*
> *Always try to match your withholding and estimated payments as close to the expected tax as possible.*

If your total payments were not more than the total tax, go to the next section titled **Amount You Owe**. On **Line 78**, subtract Line 74 from Line 63. If the amount owed is less than $1000, you paid the same amount of taxes you had owed the previous year, or you paid at least 90% of the tax due for the current year, you should not have a penalty. If you think you may owe a penalty, download Form 2210 **Underpayment of Estimated Tax** from www.irs.gov/pub/irs-pdf/f2210.pdf and follow the instructions.

Now your federal returns are complete, it's time to work on the state and local one.

Check your state's department of revenue and your municipality's website to see what the annual reporting requirements are. Besides income and sales tax reports, there may be local business reporting requirements.

### BANISH Action Steps

- **At month-end,** *finish paying the bills and download the banking and credit card transactions.*
- *Calculate your mileage deduction.*
- *Invoice customers—don't forget to include any expense that should be billed to them.*
- *Reconcile bank and credit card statements.*
- *Run financial statements and analyze for trends and concerns.*
- **At quarter-end,** *pay sales taxes and quarterly employment taxes (1040 ES).*
- **At year-end,** *send 1099s to independent contractors and the 1096 to the IRS.*
- *Reconcile 1099s received to your financial statements.*
- *Count inventory and calculate Cost of Goods Sold.*
- *Calculate depreciation.*
- *Complete the Schedule C (for sole proprietors) and Form 1040.*

*During his Senate confirmation hearing as Treasury Secretary, Timothy Geithner acknowledged he had not paid self-employment taxes for several years and had deducted his children's sleep-away camp.*

*The Treasury Secretary was charged $15,000 interest, but was not fined for the late payment.*

## BANISH Step 6—Head Into Next Year

Planning is an important part of a business, no matter the size. You shouldn't decide to drive for a ridesharing service until you understand the full impact of the costs and the revenue you can expect back. Nor should you invest in inventory for a home-based retail business until you have researched the market potential.

This is where the fun part of accounting comes in. You can set up a spreadsheet and play "What-if" games, using different scenarios of expected income and the related expenses. If you have an e-commerce website that costs $30 per month, when does it make sense to get the additional features that cost $80 per month? Will the additional expense pay for itself in new sales or upselling options? What return can you expect on Facebook ads?

These are the type of questions you need to explore as a business owner. To help you do that, use your current year's data to extrapolate what you think may happen next year. Let's assume you're a writer and you see the sales of the latest book in your series is trending lower than the previous book. Is it time to write a new story in that series or start a new series? Understanding your trends, historical costs, and the cost of changes you want to implement are keys to running and growing a successful business.

### A. Budgeting—An Annual Approach that is Your Secret Weapon

Budgeting is the estimation of expected income and expenses for a particular period of time in the future. It's not an exact science, but an exercise of using historical information and your business intuition to calculate how well you think your business will do next year.

### Banish Bite #33
*Schedule time near the end of the year to dig into the details of your financial statements and focus on what you would like to change for the next year.*

Start by setting up a spreadsheet listing your income and expense categories. The example below is from the spreadsheet program I offer for sale at www.AccountantBesideYou.com, but you can easily set up something similar yourself.

### MY BUSINESS
### BUDGET TO ACTUAL YTD

**DATE:** 02/22/17    Month #   0

Cash Beginning of Period:    $   -

| | | Actual | Budget | Linear Budget YTD | YTD Actuals | % |
|---|---|---|---|---|---|---|
| | | Previous Yr | 2017 | 22-Feb-17 | 2017 | |
| **Revenue** | | | | | | |
| 4001 | Income 1 | | | $   - | $   - | 0% |
| 4002 | Income 2 | | | $   - | $   - | 0% |
| 4003 | Income 3 | | | $   - | $   - | 0% |
| 5002 | Cost of Goods Sold type 3 | | | $   - | $   - | 0% |
| | Total Revenue: | $   - | $   - | $   - | $   - | |
| **Expenses:** | | | | | | |
| 6008 | Advertising | | | $   - | $   - | 0% |
| 6009 | Car and Truck Expenses | | | $   - | $   - | 0% |
| 6010 | Commission and Fees | | | $   - | $   - | 0% |
| 6011 | Contract Labor | | | $   - | $   - | 0% |
| 6014 | Employee Benefit Programs | | | $   - | $   - | 0% |
| 6015 | Insurance | | | $   - | $   - | 0% |
| 6016-a | Interest-Mortgage | | | $   - | $   - | 0% |
| 6016-b | Interest-Other | | | $   - | $   - | 0% |
| 6017 | Legal and Professional Services | | | $   - | $   - | 0% |
| 6018 | Office Expense | | | $   - | $   - | 0% |
| 6019 | Pension and Profit-Sharing Plans | | | $   - | $   - | 0% |
| 6020-a | Rent/Lease-Vehicle | | | $   - | $   - | 0% |
| 6020-b | Rent/Lease-Other Business | | | $   - | $   - | 0% |
| | Total Expenses: | $   - | $   - | $   - | $   - | |
| **Net : Income Gain / (Loss)** | | $   - | $   - | $   - | $   - | |
| **Cash End of Period** | | | | | $   - | |

Next populate the **Actual** column with your historical data. This may be done manually or automatically via formulas by linking data from the spreadsheet that tracks your individual transactions.

To fill in the **Budget** column, you'll want to consider whether the line item will be stable or varies with your sales volume or trends you may be seeing. I like to start with the **Expenses** because they tend to be easier to estimate.

**Overhead expenses** often stay close to the same every month or year, like rent on a storage unit or your website hosting fee. Fill those numbers in first. For expenses that vary by month like utilities or office supplies, look at your previous year's spending and make an estimate from there. Don't forget to include mileage to the post office, telephone expenses, and the like.

Examine any **one-time or "unusual" expenses**, like legal fees. Do you expect to have any in the coming year? If you are an inventor, are you considering hiring a patent attorney? Or maybe you want to incorporate your business this year; if so, estimate the fees.

If you travel to a trade show or seminars during the year, be sure to include registration fees, transportation, and meals. Using the Federal per diem rates by city is a great way to get a fairly accurate cost (see page 106).

Now let's think about the **Income**. If your market is stable and you don't expect to make many changes, you will budget your sales close to last year's. But if your website was only up for part of the year, you'll extrapolate the trend of sales for a full year impact.

If you are estimating from a partial year, be careful to consider seasonality. My accounting book sales are much higher in the first quarter of the year than over the summer months, but an average retail store does more business in the last quarter of the year for the Christmas season.

Consider if you will be adding other sources of income. Perhaps you're an artist who teaches children's art and will be offering adult classes. You will not have a historical trend to follow, so you'll need to use your best judgment for new revenues. I personally always budget a lower level of sales than I expect, so I can manage my cash flow with less chance of an unpleasant surprise.

Go back to the expenses and add any additional costs of the new source of income. The adult art class will require some advertising or promotion, additional supplies, and maybe contract labor if an additional teacher or assistant is required.

Review all the remaining expenses and look for items that vary with income level: commissions, affiliate fees, etc. Budget the dollars based on your historical trends plus or minus the expected impact of the increase or decrease of sales.

Your spreadsheet will show you the expected net income or loss for the year. Remember—this is before you take any money out for a draw or pay self-employment tax. If it's a loss, you'll need to evaluate whether you can increase revenues or decrease expenses enough to make money. If not, you must decide if it's worth your time to continue with this business.

Sometimes business will run a loss for the first year or two as they build a customer base or because of large upfront costs. By preparing a budget, you will have a better feel for how long it will take to recoup those losses and to evaluate if your time might be better spent on a different project.

Once you have a budget you feel comfortable with and understand what is included in each line item, you'll want to track your actual financial results against it. The easiest way to do this is to simply divide the annual costs by 12 and compare it to each month.

If your business is seasonal with large monthly variations of sales and expenses, you'll want to break it out to a monthly budget to track **Expected Cash Flow**. Preparing a budget by month also allows you to track when large expected expenses like travel will occur. Understanding when your cash will increase (i.e. sales received exceeds expenses paid) will allow you to plan on putting money back for the months that sales may be less than the monthly expenses (i.e. when quarterly employment taxes are due).

**Banish Bite #34**

*Consider doing a couple of versions of the budget. For the initial round, be very conservative, utilizing your historical data.*

*For the next version, consider how much you will need to spend in marketing and promotion to increase the sales.*

*And, finally, prepare a version to recognize what additional expenses may be needed to handle a large increase in sales—i.e. hiring contractors, additional warehouse space, etc.*

On the next page is the monthly budget spreadsheet offered at www.AccountantBesideYou.com. The example is for an e-commerce store that has the most sales in the last quarter of the year. Notice the entrepreneur starts out with $3000 at the beginning of the year. He expects to make $1115 during January (**Net Income** line), but must pay the self-employment taxes from last October-December's income. This brings his cash flow down to $195.

He continues to make money for the next several months, but April's self-employment taxes take his cash level to $720, and traveling to a seminar in May will cause a loss of $1410. By doing a thorough monthly budget, he knows his business account will be short of cash for the months of May and June.

Having this information gives him the foresight to invest more money into his business or to line up financing. He also sees that his cash flow will improve significantly in the last quarter, so he can plan appropriately for the following year.

Keep in mind, no matter how much thought and effort you put into designing a budget, the actual income and expenses will not match. A budget is only a tool. If the variance between expected and actual is small, you can assume your budget assumptions are still valid. If a variance is large, it's a red flag to investigate.

## MONTHLY BUDGET

DATE: ###
Beginning Cash $3,000

| | Budget January | Budget February | Budget March | Budget April | Budget May | Budget June | Budget July | Budget Au... | Budget November | Budget December | Total |
|---|---|---|---|---|---|---|---|---|---|---|---|
| **Revenue** | | | | | | | | | | | |
| Income 1 | $ 1,000 | $ 750 | $ 500 | $ 500 | $ 500 | $ 500 | $ 500 | $ | 2,500 | $ 3,000 | $13,750 |
| Income 2 | | | | | | | | | | | $ - |
| Cost of Goods Sold | $ 400 | $ 300 | $ 200 | $ 200 | $ 200 | $ 200 | $ 200 | $ | 1,000 | $ 1,200 | $ 5,500 |
| Total Revenue: | $ 1,400 | $ 1,050 | $ 700 | $ 700 | $ 700 | $ 700 | $ 700 | | 3,500 | $ 4,200 | $19,250 |
| **Expenses:** | | | | | | | | | | | |
| Advertising | $ 25 | $ 25 | $ 25 | $ 25 | $ 25 | $ 25 | $ 25 | $ | 100 | $ 100 | $ 525 |
| Car | | | | | | | | | | | $ - |
| Commissions | $ 150 | $ 113 | $ 75 | $ 75 | $ 75 | $ 75 | $ 75 | $ | $ 375 | $ 450 | $ 2,063 |
| Contract Labor | | | | | | | | | | | $ - |
| Legal | | | | | | | | | | | $ - |
| Office | $ 10 | $ 10 | $ 10 | $ 10 | $ 10 | $ 10 | $ 10 | $ | $ 20 | $ 20 | $ 150 |
| Travel | | | | | $ 500 | | | | | | $ 500 |
| Meals | | | | | $ 300 | | | | | | $ 300 |
| Utilities | $ 200 | $ 200 | $ 200 | $ 200 | $ 200 | $ 200 | $ 200 | | 200 | $ 200 | $ 2,400 |
| Wages | | | | | | | | | | | $ - |
| Seminars | | | | | $ 1,000 | | | | | | $ 1,000 |
| Total Expenses | $ 385 | $ 348 | $ 310 | $ 310 | $ 2,110 | $ 310 | $ 310 | $ | 695 | $ 770 | $ 6,938 |
| Net Income/(Loss) | $ 1,015 | $ 703 | $ 390 | $ 390 | $(1,410) | $ 390 | $ 390 | $ | 2,805 | $ 3,430 | $12,313 |

| | | | | | | | |
|---|---|---|---|---|---|---|---|
| FICA/MC | 15% | $ 1,296 | | $324.56 | (97.02) | | |
| Fed/state Inc. tax | 30% | $ 2,525 | | $ 632.25 | $ (189.0...) | | |
| Cash End of Period | $ 195 | $ 897 | $1,287 | $ 720 | $ (690) | $ (14) | $ 376 | $ ... 6,860 | $ 10,290 |

Many times, variances will be timing issues. You may have paid your monthly website fee on the 1st of the month and then on the 31st for the next month. Or perhaps, you finished a free-lancing job for a customer earlier than you expected. Your income my show higher than budget this month, but will be lower than budget next month. Timing issues are usually resolved after the next month.

Variances can also point to fraud or theft. Perhaps your office supply expense is well above budget. You examine your credit card automatic download to see money was spent on websites or at businesses you don't usually frequent. By watching this monthly, you can alert your credit card company promptly.

Sometimes you'll run over or under budget for valid business reasons. If the amount is significant, it's a good to time to reevaluate what you are doing and institute changes to increase any positive or negate any negative impact.

I've given you the basics with a spreadsheet model. Most online or desktop accounting program will include a budget feature. You'll need to enter your budget data, and the system will automatically update the actual data as it incurs.

### B. Forecasting—Evaluating as The Environment Changes

Forecasting is similar to budgeting, but is done as your business environment changes.

> *Think of the budget as the annual planning tool,*
> *and the forecast is more the "what-now" tool.*

Maybe you have an eBay store, but are wondering if you should set up your own website to expand your market and reduce the selling fees. You'll need to research the one-time costs of starting the site, i.e. web design, ecommerce options, hosting, SSL certificates, SEO optimization, etc. Next, calculate the ongoing monthly costs to maintain the site: e-commerce or cart fee, credit card processing fees, email marketing programs, marketing costs, etc. Once you have a feel for the estimated expenses, you'll see how much of an increase in gross profit (sales minus cost of goods sold) is required.

If it's reasonable to believe you can increase the sales to cover the costs over an acceptable amount of time, then start the new website. If not, you may want to do more research, find a lower cost approach, or just wait and watch your market for an opportunity later.

If you've prepared a monthly budget spreadsheet, you can use a copy to see the impact of your proposals on the current year's expected income. Key in the year-to-date actual income and expenses under the month just completed. Then adjust your remaining months for the expected changes in income and related expenses.

Sometimes you cannot increase sales without a significant increase in cost. If you have a lawn service and have as many clients as you can comfortably handle by yourself, you may have to hire an employee to add more lawns. One additional lawn is probably not enough to justify adding an employee because of all the additional costs: wages, employment taxes, benefits, payroll processing costs, additional payroll filing requirements, workman's compensation insurance, etc.

But if you want your business to grow, sometimes you have to take a leap of faith. Does hiring the employee give you some time to follow up on leads for new clients? If so, the additional costs in the short run are probably worth the risk.

You made it! Your bookkeeping is now manageable, and you have the financial tools to make great decisions. For additional tips and resources, sign up for my newsletter at **www.AccountantBesideYou.com**.

It has been my honor and pleasure to assist you on your journey. If you found the book helpful, please write a review on your favorite bookseller's website. If you have ideas on how I can improve the book, I'd love to hear from you at questions@accountantbesideyou.com.

### *Banish Action Steps*

- *Schedule time to focus on your goals for the following year.*
- *Design a budget that helps achieve those goals.*
- *Use the prior year's actual data to start your budget.*
- *Adjust the amounts for changes in sales and expenses you are expecting.*
- *Budget by month to have a strong understanding of your cash flow.*
- *Investigate any significant variances, looking for trends or problems.*
- *Use a copy of your monthly budget to forecast business opportunities for a more well-informed decision.*
- *Finally, **Go Grow Your Business!***

# Appendix

## A. Deductible Expenses from Schedule C

**Schedule C for IRS Form 1040** details the Profit or Loss From Business for a sole proprietorship. In Step 5, I showed you how to fill out the form. Here I would like to offer some details about the types of expenses that fall into the expense categories.

**Line 8 Advertising**—the total amount paid for promotional expenses. This includes business cards, advertisements, flyers, brochures, trade show costs, etc. If you have a home-based cosmetic business, the decorations and refreshments for the sales event would be charged here. If you are a writer, bookmarks handed out at a signing would be an advertising expense. If you have a booth at an event and are charged a percentage of your sales, it would go here.

Any monthly internet, hosting, and website fees are considered utilities, not advertising, and shown on Line 25.

**Line 9 Car and truck expenses**—expenses are based either on a standard rate for mileage (see www.IRS.gov for the current rate) or actual expenses if the vehicle was used more than half the time for the business. I recommend using the standard rate as you simply need to track the mileage used for business instead of keeping track of all the receipts and costs and then calculating the percentage.

If you are participating in a ride-sharing service, you may deduct your miles to pick up your fare customers as well the time they are in the car. If you are putting substantial miles on your car, you may wish to track the actual expenses to see if the deduction would be higher. Actual car expenses allowed by the IRS are: depreciation or lease payments, licenses, gas, oil, tolls, insurance, garage rent, parking fees, registration fees, repairs, and tires.

If the car is not dedicated to the business, you'll also need to fill out Part IV of Schedule C (Lines 43-47) showing the miles driven for business versus personal and answer a few questions.

| **Part IV** | Information on Your Vehicle. Complete this part **only** if you are claiming car or truck expenses on line 9 and are not required to file Form 4562 for this business. See the instructions for line 13 to find out if you must file Form 4562. |
|---|---|

43  When did you place your vehicle in service for business purposes? (month, day, year) ▶ ...... / ...... / ......

44  Of the total number of miles you drove your vehicle during 2016, enter the number of miles you used your vehicle for:

a  Business ........................ b  Commuting (see instructions) ........................ c  Other ........................

45  Was your vehicle available for personal use during off-duty hours? . . . . . . . . . . . . . ☐ Yes ☐ No

46  Do you (or your spouse) have another vehicle available for personal use?. . . . . . . . . . . ☐ Yes ☐ No

47a  Do you have evidence to support your deduction? . . . . . . . . . . . . . . . . . ☐ Yes ☐ No

b  If "Yes," is the evidence written? . . . . . . . . . . . . . . . . . . . . . ☐ Yes ☐ No

**BANISH Bite # 35**

*If you want to deduct car expenses or mileage, you MUST keep track of the miles driven for business. Keep a notebook in your glove compartment or put an app on your phone that uses your GPS to track trips, like MileIQ or QuickBooks Self-Employed. Don't forget to record the business purpose.*

**Line 10 Commissions and fees**—if you paid someone to sell your products. It may also be used for fees paid to other businesses that are not professional or contract labor; i.e. a writer or artist may hire a publicity company. Check to make sure there are not more appropriate categories before using this one.

**Line 11 Contract labor**—this is where you charge the labor that may have required 1099s. We discussed this in detail in Step 5.

**Line 12 Depletion**—per the IRS: *Depletion is the using up of natural resources by mining, drilling, quarrying stone, or cutting timber. The depletion deduction allows an owner or operator to account for the reduction of a product's reserves.*

As it is unlikely you'll need it, let's consider it outside the scope of this book.

**Line 13 Depreciation and Section 179**—this is where you expense large purchases (capital expenditures in accountant talk) over several years. Check back in Step 5 for more details.

**Line 14 Employee Benefit Programs**—for the scope of this book, I'm assuming you are self-employed without employees or their related benefits. I'll be writing a BANISH book for small businesses soon to address these issues.

**Line 15 Insurance (other than Health)**—this is for your business insurance only (general liability or specific business policies), not homeowner's insurance. If you have an outside office, insurance on it and the contents can go here. If you have a home office, the renters or homeowner's insurance is part of the home office deduction.

**Line 16 Interest-Mortgage & Other**—there are two lines here—(a)and (b). Line 16 (a) is designated for mortgage interest on property used for the business. If you took out a loan against your house to fund the business, you deduct it here instead of with your personal itemized deductions. Your regular mortgage interest on your house is not deductible on this line if you did not take out a separate loan for the business. You should receive a Form 1098 from your bank for the amount.

Line 16 (b) is for other interest charges like credit card interest, though I hope you are managing your cash flow so you won't have much of this.

**Line 17 Legal and professional services**—your attorney and accountant fees go here. This includes any incorporation or set-up fees and fees for tax advice and preparation. Hopefully, by reading this book, the expense will be low.

**Line 18 Office Expense**—office paper, pens, printer ink or toner, calendars, postage, and other miscellaneous office supplies go here. Supplies related to your business or products (not the administrative functions) go on Line 22 Supplies.

### BANISH Bite # 36

*Because Office Expense can be such a catch-all category, take care not to charge personal items or large expenditures here.*

*For example, a $50 computer keyboard can be considered an office expense, but a $1000 laptop needs to be depreciated.*

*(Remember the capital expenditure/depreciation conversation we had in Step 5?)*

**Line 19 Pension and Profit Sharing**—there are options to set up a one-participant retirement plan which requires also filing Form 5500-EZ. Check with your local CPA on the current options and regulations.

**Line 20 Rent or Lease-Vehicles, machinery vs other property**—put the amount of rent for any vehicles or machinery on Line 20(a). If you leased a vehicle for 30 or more days, there is an additional calculation required to reduce the deduction by the "inclusion" amount. IRS Publication 463 explains how to calculate the inclusion www.irs.gov/pub/irs-pdf/p463.pdf.

Rent on office, production, or warehouse space is recorded on Line 20b.

**Line 21 Repairs & Maintenance**—record costs to maintain or repair your work space and equipment here. If the work is substantial enough to improve the value of the property, it's not a repair and maintenance expense; it is a capital expenditure. For example, let's say the roof on your dedicated storage shed starts to leak. You climb to the top and replace a few shingles. You can deduct the expense of the shingles, but not your labor. If you hire someone else to replace the shingles, their labor is deductible. If, on the other hand, while you have some of the shingles off, you decide to expand the building, the cost needs to be capitalized and depreciated over several years.

**Line 22 Supplies**—these are supplies related to your products or business that you consumed over the course of the year, not office supplies. Books used for research or technical manuals, small equipment, and professional instruments are also expensed on Line 22. For example, an artist would charge their brushes, paints, canvases, and cleaning liquids and rags here.

**Line 23 Taxes and Licenses**—we know there will always be death and taxes. This line will reflect the following:

- State and local sales tax paid to the governmental agency on your sales. The tax you collected from the buyer must be included in the gross sales on Line 1.
- Real estate and personal property taxes on the BUSINESS assets.
- The employer's share of Social Security and Medicare taxes.
- Federal and state unemployment tax (FUTA/SUTA).
- Federal highway use tax.
- One half of your self-employment tax on Form 1040 Line 27.

Line 23 is not the place for:

- Federal income tax
- Estate and gift taxes
- Taxes assessed for improvements (e.g. paving, sewers)
- Taxes on your home or personal property
- Sales tax paid on the property you purchased for your business. These taxes are treated as part of the property cost and expensed in the appropriate categories.
- Any other taxes and license fees not related to your business.

**Line 24(a) Travel**—remember, this is only for business trips. If you take a spouse or child, their expenses are NOT deductible. This line includes flights, tips, parking, taxis, and hotels. Meals and entertainment are shown on Line 24 (b). If you will be deducting travel expenses, I highly recommend filling out an expense report (templates are available in most word processing programs) documenting the dates, expenses, and business need for each of these trips. Don't be afraid to link pictures and websites to the reports if they help explain the business purpose.

Remember the deductibility rule: **Necessary and Reasonable**. If you're a writer and think it's necessary to go to the Virgin Islands for inspiration, I'm afraid the IRS would not consider that reasonable.

On the other hand, if you are writing a travel book about the Virgin Islands, you have a case to argue. Be sure to differentiate your pleasure days from your research days, and only deduct the portion of the necessary travel.

**Line 24 (b) Deductible meals & entertainment**—are those related to taking your clients or business associates out for dinner or entertainment. These expenses have a limit. Currently only 50% of the expense can be deducted. You also must write the customer or associates name on the receipt and the business purpose.

If you are traveling, you may consider using the Federal Per Diem Rates.

---

### BANISH Bite #37

*You may find it to your advantage to use the Federal Per Diem Rates for your meals and incidentals. These are determined annually by the government. Go to www.gsa.gov to search these rates by state and city.*

*The M&IE rates are broken out by meal and $5 a day for incidentals like tips for porters.*

*If you use the standard rates, the first and last day of travel are calculated at 75% of the Federal Per Diem Rate.*

---

Meals purchased on overnight travel are also only 50% deductible, whether you use actual expenses or the per diem rates.

The Entertainment portion of this line includes activities you attended with your client, like a sporting event or play. You must note who you took and the business discussed at the event.

If you purchase tickets to an industry event, perhaps tickets to the local craft show you will have a booth at, and give them to customers or vendors to attend, this would be considered a promotional cost. Then it would be fully deductible.

**Line 25 Utilities**—are for your office space, shop, or warehouse if you have separate facilities from your house. These include water, electricity, gas, trash pickup etc. If your office is in your home, the expenses will be recorded on Line 30, as we discussed on page 84.

Telephone and internet expenses used for business purposes go here. This could be the cost of a second phone line or your business cell phone. You can't deduct the cost of your primary home phone, but you're allowed to charge the business-related long distance calls. If your business requires you to have a smart phone (i.e. a rideshare driver), you can deduct the percentage of your data used for the business as an expense, even if it's your only phone.

Website site hosting fees also go here.

**Line 26 Wages**—for purposes of this book, I'm assuming you do not have employees. But if you do, this is where you would record their salaries or wages. This is NOT the place to put any money paid to you as the owner.

If you have any expenses on this line, you are required to file a Form W-2 (Wage and Tax Statement) for each employee.

**Line 27 (a)—Other Expenses: Those Not Detailed on Schedule C**

Quite possibly, you will have expenses that do not fit into the categories listed on Lines 8-26. Any expenses specific to your business not already listed will go on Page 2 of **Schedule C**, **Part V—Other Expenses**. There are nine lines on the form, but if you have more, you can write "See Attached" and include a separate schedule of expenses.

Expenses often seen in this area are: bad debts from customers not paying their bills, start-up expenses up to $5,000 (see Publication 535 for details), and amortization of trademark costs, and research and development. Other typical expenses would be costs of licenses required for your profession or business, seminars, dues to organizations, and subscriptions.

Do NOT include personal or family expenses, charitable contributions (these will be included on your Form 1040, Schedule A—Itemized Deductions if you aren't using the standard deduction), or any fines or penalties paid to a government agency.

# B. Home Office Deductions

If you regularly conduct business from your home and have a room or part of a room dedicated to business use, there is a home office deduction available on Schedule C, Line 30.

As discussed on page 84, there are two methods to calculate your home office deduction—the **Simplified Method** and **Form 8829 Expenses for Business Use of Your Home**. The Simplified Method is substantially easier to calculate. In the **Schedule C Instructions**, there is a **Simplified Method Worksheet** (www.irs.gov/instructions/i1040sc/ch02.html#d0e1077).

**Simplified Method Worksheet**                                    *Keep for Your Records*

1. Enter the amount of the gross income limitation. See Instructions for the Simplified Method Worksheet .............. 1. _____

2. Allowable square footage for the qualified business use. Do not enter more than 300 square feet. See Instructions for the Simplified Method Worksheet ......................................... 2. _____

3. Simplified method amount
   a. Maximum allowable amount ................................................... 3a. ___$5___
   b. For daycare facilities not used exclusively for business, enter the decimal amount from the Daycare Facility Worksheet; otherwise, enter 1.0 ................................. 3b. _____
   c. Multiply line 3a by line 3b and enter result to 2 decimal places ............................ 3c. _____

4. Multiply line 2 by line 3c ......................................................... 4. _____

5. **Allowable expenses using the simplified method.** Enter the smaller of line 1 or line 4 here and include that amount on Schedule C, line 30. If zero or less, enter -0- ................................. 5. _____

6. **Carryover of unallowed expenses from 2015 that are not allowed in 2016.**
   a. Operating expenses. Enter the amount from your 2015 Form 8829, line 42 ................... 6a. _____
   b. Excess casualty losses and depreciation. Enter the amount from your 2015 Form 8829, line 43 ................ 6b. _____

**Instructions for the Simplified Method Worksheet**

Use this worksheet to figure the amount of expenses you may deduct for a qualified business use of a home if you are electing to use the simplified method for that home. If you are not electing to use the simplified method, use Form 8829.

**Line 1.** If all gross income from your trade or business is from this qualified business use of your home, figure your gross income limitation as follows.

A. Enter the amount from Schedule C, line 29 ............................................. _____
B. Enter any gain derived from the business use of your home and shown on Form 8949 (and included on Schedule D) or Form 4797 ..... _____
C. Add lines A and B ................................................................ _____
D. Enter the loss (as a positive number) shown on Form 8949 (and included on Schedule D) or Form 4797 that are allocable to the business, but not allocable to the use of the home ............................................................ _____
E. Gross income limitation. Subtract line D from line C. Enter the result here and on line 1 ........................ _____

**Line 1** asks for your gross income limitation. This is calculated on the second part of the worksheet and includes your Schedule C, Line 29 income the Sales of Capital Assets (Form 8949) and Sales of Business Property (Form 4797). I'm going to assume you won't have these, so put the Tentative profit or loss from Line 29.

**Line 2** is the square footage of space you wish to deduct, up to 300 square feet.

**Line 3** shows the rate per square foot as $5 unless you are running a day care. If so, follow the IRS instructions.

**Line 4** calculates the deduction by multiplying $5 times the square footage.

**Line 5** compares the calculation to your gross income limitation on Line 1. You cannot deduct more home office expense than your tentative net income plus gain on sales of business assets. Enter the smaller number on Line 30 of Schedule C.

**Line 6** is used only if you used the longer home office Form 8829 last year and could not use all the expenses.

The simplified method does not include depreciation on your house. If you think your deduction could be significantly larger, fill out **Form 8829** and compare your deductions.

| Form **8829** | **Expenses for Business Use of Your Home** | OMB No. 1545-0074 |
|---|---|---|
| Department of the Treasury Internal Revenue Service (99) | ▶ File only with Schedule C (Form 1040). Use a separate Form 8829 for each home you used for business during the year. ▶ Information about Form 8829 and its separate instructions is at *www.irs.gov/form8829*. | **2016** Attachment Sequence No. **176** |
| Name(s) of proprietor(s) | | Your social security number |

**Part I    Part of Your Home Used for Business**

| | | | |
|---|---|---|---|
| 1 | Area used regularly and exclusively for business, regularly for daycare, or for storage of inventory or product samples (see instructions) . . . . . . . . . . . . . . . . | **1** | |
| 2 | Total area of home . . . . . . . . . . . . . . . . . . . . . | **2** | |
| 3 | Divide line 1 by line 2. Enter the result as a percentage . . . . . . . . . . . | **3** | % |
| | For daycare facilities not used exclusively for business, go to line 4. All others, go to line 7. | | |
| 4 | Multiply days used for daycare during year by hours used per day | **4** | hr. |
| 5 | Total hours available for use during the year (366 days x 24 hours) (see instructions) | **5** | 8,784 hr. |
| 6 | Divide line 4 by line 5. Enter the result as a decimal amount . . . | **6** | . |
| 7 | Business percentage. For daycare facilities not used exclusively for business, multiply line 6 by line 3 (enter the result as a percentage). All others, enter the amount from line 3 . . . . . ▶ | **7** | % |

**Part II    Figure Your Allowable Deduction**

| | | | (a) Direct expenses | (b) Indirect expenses | |
|---|---|---|---|---|---|
| 8 | Enter the amount from Schedule C, line 29, plus any gain derived from the business use of your home, minus any loss from the trade or business not derived from the business use of your home (see instructions) | **8** | | | |
| | See instructions for columns (a) and (b) before completing lines 9–21. | | | | |
| 9 | Casualty losses (see instructions). . . . . | **9** | | | |
| 10 | Deductible mortgage interest (see instructions) | **10** | | | |
| 11 | Real estate taxes (see instructions) . . . . | **11** | | | |
| 12 | Add lines 9, 10, and 11 . . . . . . . . | **12** | | | |
| 13 | Multiply line 12, column (b) by line 7 . . . . | | **13** | | |
| 14 | Add line 12, column (a) and line 13 . . . . | | | **14** | |
| 15 | Subtract line 14 from line 8. If zero or less, enter -0- | | | **15** | |
| 16 | Excess mortgage interest (see instructions) . | **16** | | | |
| 17 | Insurance . . . . . . . . . . . . . | **17** | | | |
| 18 | Rent . . . . . . . . . . . . . . | **18** | | | |
| 19 | Repairs and maintenance . . . . . . . | **19** | | | |
| 20 | Utilities . . . . . . . . . . . . . | **20** | | | |
| 21 | Other expenses (see instructions). . . . . | **21** | | | |
| 22 | Add lines 16 through 21 . . . . . . . . | **22** | | | |
| 23 | Multiply line 22, column (b) by line 7 . . . . | | **23** | | |
| 24 | Carryover of prior year operating expenses (see instructions) . . | | **24** | | |
| 25 | Add line 22, column (a), line 23, and line 24 . . . . . . . . . . | | | **25** | |
| 26 | Allowable operating expenses. Enter the **smaller** of line 15 or line 25 . . . . . . . . . . | | | **26** | |
| 27 | Limit on excess casualty losses and depreciation. Subtract line 26 from line 15 . . . . . | | | **27** | |
| 28 | Excess casualty losses (see instructions) . . . . . . . . . | **28** | | | |
| 29 | Depreciation of your home from line 41 below . . . . . . . . . | **29** | | | |
| 30 | Carryover of prior year excess casualty losses and depreciation (see instructions) . . . . . . . . . . . . . . . . . . | **30** | | | |
| 31 | Add lines 28 through 30 . . . . . . . . . . . . . . . . . . . . . | | | **31** | |
| 32 | Allowable excess casualty losses and depreciation. Enter the **smaller** of line 27 or line 31 . . | | | **32** | |
| 33 | Add lines 14, 26, and 32. . . . . . . . . . . . . . . . . . . . . | | | **33** | |
| 34 | Casualty loss portion, if any, from lines 14 and 32. Carry amount to **Form 4684** (see instructions) | | | **34** | |
| 35 | **Allowable expenses for business use of your home.** Subtract line 34 from line 33. Enter here and on Schedule C, line 30. If your home was used for more than one business, see instructions ▶ | | | **35** | |

**Part III    Depreciation of Your Home**

| | | | |
|---|---|---|---|
| 36 | Enter the **smaller** of your home's adjusted basis or its fair market value (see instructions) . . | **36** | |
| 37 | Value of land included on line 36 . . . . . . . . . . . . . . . . . . | **37** | |
| 38 | Basis of building. Subtract line 37 from line 36 . . . . . . . . . . . . . | **38** | |
| 39 | Business basis of building. Multiply line 38 by line 7 . . . . . . . . . . . . . . | **39** | |
| 40 | Depreciation percentage (see instructions) . . . . . . . . . . . . . . . . . | **40** | % |
| 41 | Depreciation allowable (see instructions). Multiply line 39 by line 40. Enter here and on line 29 above | **41** | |

**Part IV    Carryover of Unallowed Expenses to 2017**

| | | | |
|---|---|---|---|
| 42 | Operating expenses. Subtract line 26 from line 25. If less than zero, enter -0- . . . . . | **42** | |
| 43 | Excess casualty losses and depreciation. Subtract line 32 from line 31. If less than zero, enter -0- | **43** | |

For Paperwork Reduction Act Notice, see your tax return instructions.      Cat. No. 13232M      Form **8829** (2016)

# About the Author

**Lisa London, CPA** is known worldwide as **The Accountant Beside You**. She has spent three decades working in public accounting as an auditor and small business consultant with Deloitte & Touche, LLP, in corporate accounting as a director of finance for a division of Kodak, Inc., and as a consultant with venture capital and small businesses and nonprofits.

She began writing her books after helping her church with an accounting system conversion. Lisa found very limited resources to help the office staff and volunteers understand their basic accounting requirements. She realized that if her church needed guidance, other churches probably did too.

That aha moment led her to create **The Accountant Beside You** series of resources. Her first book, *QuickBooks for Churches and Other Religious Organizations,* is being used on six continents and has been translated into Spanish.

When she's not working on accounting books or spending time with her husband and four children, Lisa enjoys sneaking away to write historical fiction. Her debut novel, *Darker the Night,* which tells the story of a young woman growing up in Hitler's Germany from the perspective of a German civilian, has become a popular selection for book clubs.

# Acknowledgments

As always, it takes a tremendous amount of help to write a book. The assistance of my editor, S.P. Sipal, was invaluable. Once again, Greg Schultz designed a phenomenal cover. Martha Bullen's advice was always spot on.

My contributors, Terressa Pierce and Abby Eisenkraft, were generous with their time and advice, as were all my early readers.

I also need to thank my family for their patience and ability to humor me as I made them listen to "just one more" great idea for the book.

And thanks goes to you, my reader. I hope you have found the book helpful. Feel free to go to www.accountantbesideyou.com with questions or to post ideas that work for you on the discussion page.

If you found the book useful, please help me assist other small businesses by writing a review on your favorite bookseller site and by sharing a post on your social media.

Thanks, and happy accounting!

*Lisa London*

# Resources

| Description | Website |
|---|---|
| **IRS** | |
| General Site—Use search box for forms/topics | www.IRS.Gov |
| Hobby vs Business | www.irs.gov/uac/is-your-hobby-a-for-profit-endeavor |
| Publication 505 Tax Withholding & Estimated Tax | www.irs.gov/pub/irs-pdf/p505.pdf |
| 2017 Tax Withholding Rates | www.irs.gov/pub/irs-pdf/n1036.pdf |
| Form 1040 Estimated Tax for Individuals | www.irs.gov/pub/irs-pdf/f1040es.pdf |
| Direct Pay | www.irs.gov/payments/direct-pay |
| Request for Taxpayer Identification Number (for Independent Contractors) | www.irs.gov/pub/irs-pdf/fw9.pdf |
| Order Free Forms | www.irs.gov/businesses/online-ordering-for-information-returns-and-employer-returns |
| Form 1099-MISC Miscellaneous Income | www.irs.gov/pub/irs-pdf/f1099msc.pdf |
| Form 4562 Depreciation and Amortization | www.irs.gov/uac/about-form-4562 |
| Principal Business or Professional Activity Code | www.irs.gov/instructions/i1040sc/ch02.html#d0e2016 |
| Form 8829 Expenses for Business Use of Your Home | www.irs.gov/pub/irs-pdf/f8829.pdf |

| Description | Website |
|---|---|
| Home Office Deduction Simplified | www.irs.gov/instructions/i1040sc/ch02.html#d0e1077 |
| Form 1040 Schedule SE | www.irs.gov/pub/irs-pdf/i1040sse.pdf |
| Form 2210 Underpayment of Estimated Tax | www.irs.gov/pub/irs-pdf/f2210.pdf |
| Publication 535 Business Expenses | www.irs.gov/uac/about-publication-535 |
| Publication 463 Travel, Entertainment, Gift, and Car Expenses | www.irs.gov/pub/irs-pdf/p463.pdf |
| Publication 583 Starting a Business and Keeping Records | www.irs.gov/pub/irs-pdf/p583.pdf |
| **GSA** Per Diem Rates | www.gsa.gov |
| **State Dept. of Revenue & Secretaries of State** | www.accountantbesideyou.com/state-weblinks |
| **Software/Apps** | |
| Full accounting package: desktop and online | Quickbooks.intuit.com |
| Full accounting package: online | Xero.com/us |
| Full accounting package: online | Waveapps.com |
| Home and Business: desktop and smartphone | Quicken.com |
| Personal: online | Mint.com |
| Smartphone app | Quickbooks.intuit.com/Self-Employed |

| Description | Website |
|---|---|
| Facilitate bill paying | Bill.com |
| Track mileage | Mileiq.com |
| **Other References** | |
| *101 Ways to Stay off the IRS Radar*, by Abby Eisenkraft | www.reallifetaxadvice.com |
| Terressa Pierce | www.freechurchforms.com |
| *Church Accounting—The How-To Guide for Small & Growing Churches*, by Lisa London and Vickey Boatright | www.accountantbesideyou.com/capaperback |
| *Small Nonprofits QuickBooks Primer*, by Poppy Davis, CPA | |

# Index

90250705R00068

Made in the USA
Columbia, SC
01 March 2018